Doctoral Degree Quest: A Personal Academic Passion

Completing Your Doctoral Thesis in a Timely Manner

Dr. Sherman N. Miller

S.N. Miller of Delaware, Ltd. 2010

Published in the United States of America

By SNM Publishing

A division of S.N. Miller of Delaware, Ltd.

2006 N. Van Buren Street, Wilmington, Delaware 19802

Library of Congress Cataloging-in-Publication Data

Miller, Sherman N., 1942-

Completing Your Doctoral Thesis (Dissertation)

Doctoral Degree Quest: completing your doctoral thesis (dissertation) in a timely manner / Sherman N. Miller.

Contents

Executive Summary

There is an estimated 50% attrition rate for doctoral degree candidates, so the present work offers some techniques for completing the doctoral thesis or dissertation in a timely manner. The focus is on getting writers to develop a mindset for writing and to avoid stressors that encumber one's writing ability.

The underpinning goal is to develop neighborhood role models with whom inner-city neighborhood people may interact daily and who will be indicators to the economic mainstream that there is untapped human resource potential being wasted in inner-city America. The quest of a 70-year-old inner-city senior citizen neighborhood role model, who underwent two heart surgeries in the same day during her doctoral quest, helps to dissuade impulses to give up when things appear futile.

Stories of individuals who completed the doctorate degree offer some feel for the scope of the quest the doctoral candidate is undertaking. These stories highlight pitfalls and what these individuals did or did not do to complete their doctoral degrees. The stories' slant is on people who overcame adverse predicaments to earn their doctoral degrees.

A writing template is offered that gives a framework to help university graduate students and social scientists in the development of their theses, dissertations, reports, presentations, or book manuscripts. Variants of this template have been used to generate internal corporate technical reports, trade presentations, articles for trade journals, and presentations to trade societies.

A key goal is to offer busy professionals ideas on life-style arrangements to get their writing assignments completed so that they have a significant impact on their long-term socioeconomic development. Rapid writing is implicit in the writing template, the key focus is on the completion of the doctoral thesis or dissertation and writing various corporate reports in a timely manner.

A set of adages is offered as rules of thumb that would-be thesis, dissertation and report writers will want to consider as guidelines in their quests to complete their writing tasks. These adages center on a disciplined mindset that encourages writers to finish their writing assignments instead of falling victim to an enchantment with procrastination. Writers should select the adages they feel are apropos to their immediate needs.

There is a recommendation letter with key things for a person contemplating a decision to begin the doctoral degree quest to consider.

Dedications

Mrs. Gwynelle W. Miller

I am grateful to my wife of 45 years for offering encouragement and moral support during my doctoral degree quest. Gwynelle also has been my editor for roughly 600 newspaper editorials and three books.

Mrs. Sammye E. Traudt

I thank Sammye for offering editorial upgrades to technical trade articles and reports, and for editing my manuscript on teaching business calculus, which was the key appendix in my doctoral thesis.

Ms. Shanda Wilder

I thank Ms. Shanda Wilder for her editorial comments on this work from the perspective of a potential candidate for the doctoral degree.

Reverend Dr. Zenobia A. James

I thank Reverend James for becoming my first neighborhood role model using the ideas reported in this book. Rev. James has lived in the same inner city neighborhood in the city of Wilmington, Delaware for roughly 45 years, which is a financially challenged section of the city. Although she underwent two heart surgeries in the same day, Rev. James never took her mind off of achieving her doctoral quest, which she completed under my mentorship in June 2008 at 70 years old. She is now a clear symbol of the significant untapped human resource potential in the Wilmington inner city neighborhoods.

Introduction

A middle-aged lady shared that commencing her pursuit of the doctoral degree was a bone-chilling experience. She said the speaker addressing the first meeting of her fellow doctorate-seeking students told them that there was a 60 percent attrition rate of students who attempt to earn the doctoral degree for various reasons. It was apparent that this speaker was exploiting some form of shock treatment to start the weeding-out process and to scare away any student who may harbor any doubt on his or her commitment to the tough journey that lay ahead. I wanted to discard this speaker's comments as some form of elitism until I came to recognize that this figure is not farfetched based on reports in the literature. Barbara E. Lovitts and Cary Nelson write about forty years of data that offers some legitimacy to this speaker's doctoral degree attrition claim.

Barbara E. Lovitts and Cary Nelson contend, "Historically, graduate programs have been astonishingly wasteful of their human capital. Although comprehensive national data do not exist on the consequences of graduate students' abandoning their degree programs, forty years of studies suggest the long-term attrition rate nationwide is about 50 percent" (Lovitts, 2000).

This high attrition rate calls into question the differences between people who complete the doctoral degree and those people who drop out along the way. An immediate consideration may be the significant academic performance differences between the two groups. Lovitts and Nelson also report, "The Lovitts survey found no meaningful difference between the undergraduate grade point averages of the students who did complete the Ph.D. and those who did not. The only notable difference in grade point averages surfaces when the students are separated by gender: female-completer, 3.57; non-completer, 3.62; male-completer, 3.52; non-completer, 3.49. In other words, women who abandoned graduate study had a somewhat higher undergraduate grade point average than those who stayed. What's more, women leave in higher numbers, thus suggesting once again that attrition is due to something other than ability."

Ashley Terletzky also touches on this 50 percent attrition rate and offers some rationale. "Attrition rates among doctoral candidates have become an overwhelming problem throughout the country, with rates hovering above 50 percent at many universities, including NYU. The high dropout rate has been attributed to intense workloads, high costs and isolated work environments" (Terletzky, 2004).

Terletzky further reports on the battle line between those entrenched in maintaining an elitist society of doctoral degree holders and those who recognize that the high attrition rates have national implications beyond protecting the purity of the doctoral ranks. ". . . NYU's graduate schools are battling nationwide attrition rates that are so staggering that Pfizer, a pharmaceutical corporation, donated a $2 million grant to the Council of Graduate Schools for experiments on reducing attrition, said Daniel Denecke, director of best practices for the council. . . . Some professors argue that attrition rates are healthy, because it shows that the programs eliminate those who are not up to snuff . . ."

The exclusivity of the doctoral degree club is evident in the number of degrees awarded over the last eighty years relative to the size of the U.S. population. In the period 1920 - 1999, 1,354,873 doctoral degrees were awarded in all fields as reported by Lori

Thurgood, Mary J. Gollada, and Susan T. Hill for the National Science Foundation (Thurgood, Golladay, & Hill, U.S. Doctorates in the 20th Century, 2006). Compared to the US population of 303,651,142 as reported by the U.S. Census Bureau Population Clock on December 22, 2007 at 16:34 GMT (Bureau, 2006), it confirms that doctoral degree holders are a very small portion of the population. Thurgood et al also reported, "In 1999 U.S. institutions awarded 41,140 doctorate degrees; 25,953 in S&E Fields (Science and Engineering) and 15,187 in non-S&E fields." The U.S. Census Bureau estimated the 1999 US population at 272,690,813 as of July 1, 1999 (Historical National Population Estimates: July 1, 1900 to July 1, 1999). These accounts clearly indicate that people earning doctoral degrees are an academically elite group of citizens who contribute a significant amount to the scientific and social advancements made in the world today. It should be noted that many people without doctoral degrees also make many major contributions to the body of knowledge that leads towards the betterment of humanity.

Evelyn Hunt Ogden suggests a probability of success for today's doctoral graduate student. "In 2001 there were over 200,000 academic doctoral students in 539 graduate study institutions in the United States: of those, only 44,744 were awarded degrees. It took the median doctoral student 7.6 years of enrolled time to earn the degree (National Center for Educational Statistics 2004). . . Why should it take so long? What is even more frightening than the statistics is a growing acceptance on the part of graduate students that the degree process should take up a major portion of their lives!" (Ogden, 2007)

Ogden's comment on the graduate students' view of their lot in life, coupled with Treletzky's comment on professorial recalcitrance by some professors viewing the weeding out of graduate students as the doctoral degree pursuit norm, suggest the need of a cultural change in the mindset for some professors who are guiding doctoral students' academic progress. John P. Kotter offers, "Culture changes only after you have successfully altered people's actions, after the new behavior produces some group benefit for a period of time, and after people see the connection between the new actions and the performance improvement" (Kotter, 1996).

Graduate Dean Theda Skocpol at Harvard University has become a catalyst for destroying the model of having long-tenured doctoral candidates by making these students a liability to their academic department. "A series of new policies in the humanities and the social sciences at Harvard University are premised on the idea that professors need the ticking clock, too. For the last two years, the university has announced that for every five graduate students in years eight or higher of a Ph.D. program, the department would lose one admissions slot for a new doctoral student. The results were immediate: In numerous departments that for years had large clusters of Ph.D. students taking eight or more years to finish, professors reached out to students and doctorates were completed" (Jaschik, 2007).

Skocpol said, "People get lost. Being a graduate student can end up being a very lonely experience. You've got this enormous dissertation to write, and your children are born and your partner wants you to get a new job. . . Losing somebody from one of these very selective Ph.D. programs after the investment of many years of faculty and student time and the students' own life and after we've invested a quarter million dollars of Harvard's money is really tragic."

Skocpol's effort at Harvard may pervade the national psyche, for it is in line with the need perceived by Pfizer and perhaps other corporations to produce the right human resources for them to remain viable in the twenty-first century. I project that time-to-doctoral-degree may become a significant metric in deciding what projects get governmental, foundation, and corporate sponsors in the not-too-distant future.

Hence, I will turn my attention to a discussion of ideas that doctoral candidates may find useful in enhancing their chances of completing their doctoral degree program. The initial discussion will be underpinned by comments from people who shared their doctoral candidacy experiences en route to their doctoral degrees. The presentation will shift focus to some techniques on writing the doctoral thesis or dissertation in a timely manner that are supported by my personal experiences in writing over 600 newspaper editorials, technical articles, and internal technical progress reports during my technical marketing and end use research tenure at the DuPont Company. These writing techniques have also been used in writing books for publications in the education industry.

I found that while teaching a full load of college mathematics courses, these techniques allowed me to write and defend my doctoral thesis in roughly a seven month time span. One of my thesis appendices is a standalone book replete with equations on how to teach finite mathematics and business calculus to background deficient college student populations. The writing techniques will not only help you in writing your doctoral thesis or dissertation, but also aid you in quickly writing white papers, articles, and books for publication once you land that teaching, industry or public sector job.

Chapter I

Key Issues in Degree Completion

I see the completion of the doctoral degree as an academic calling characterized by seven matters the graduate student needs to control to achieve her or his dream.

1. A *firm belief* in her or his ability to accomplish the goal.

2. An honest assessment of the *time required* to complete the doctoral degree.

3. Sources of *financial support* (grants, fellowships, gifts, loans, and corporate and non-corporate education vouchers.

4. To *think as a doctoral peer.*

5. To demonstrate *academic tenacity* in the presence of countervailing forces.

6. To avoid *academic servitude.*

7. To *cope with the doctoral committee politics*, so one does not become a pawn in political struggles between committee members.

Firm Belief

When you have been accepted to a doctoral program at a university or institution, it implies that you are thought of as having the capability to obtain the doctorate degree. Your academic wherewithal is premised to be satisfactory for your doctoral quest, so how you manage your belief in yourself under stressful conditions is the real issue to consider. Once you complete your course work, you find yourself confronted with two hurdles that may decide the fate of your doctoral degree quest: you are expected now to produce publication-caliber research and write a doctoral thesis or dissertation that documents your contribution to your field of study. The university gives you the status of All But Dissertation and you can now use its initialism ABD to share your academic status. Carnegie Mellon University Doctoral Candidate Policies for All But Dissertation (ABD) is a guide on your new status.

"After the completion of all formal degree requirements other than the completion of and approval of the doctoral dissertation and the public final examination, doctoral candidates shall be regarded as All But Dissertation (ABD). Achieving ABD status is verified by the candidate's home department. Once a student meets department criteria, ABD status must be certified by the department in writing to Enrollment Services.

"Once students achieve ABD status, their doctoral degree candidacy shall continue for a maximum of seven full academic years, unless terminated earlier by conferral of the degree, by academic or administrative action, or by a lapse of candidacy due to more restrictive department or college policy. At the expiration of the seven-year period, candidacy status shall lapse. Once candidacy has lapsed, the person may resume work towards a doctoral degree only if newly admitted to a currently offered doctoral degree program under criteria determined by that program." (All But Dissertation (ABD) Policies, 1995)

The Carnegie Mellon University ABD policy allows you to understand that pursuing the doctoral degree is not an open-ended process. This means that you want to clearly understand what your research advisor wants you to do to complete your degree. When you start to consider publishable research, you are not merely mimicking what is published by others, which may have been acceptable at the Masters Degree level. Hence, you need to have faith in your own novel ideas that offer new insights, discoveries, or directions.

A retirement-age Indian gentleman shared how it was necessary for him to truly believe in his research direction for his doctoral degree. He researched to produce a new component in a car for a multinational automobile company and produced three prototypes, all of which were unsuccessful. He says his faith in the idea was truly being tested. His fourth try was successful; therefore he got his PhD. When asked what made him continue with his research direction, he replied, "I had faith in the idea." Today he is an adjunct Professor at universities in the state of Pennsylvania.

A senior citizen chemist obtained his Bachelor of Science (BS) degree in 1960, Masters Degree in 1962 and doctorate degree in 1965, all in chemistry from a very large university. This scientist argued that once he graduated, he found that the Masters Degree was not very useful in chemistry-related positions, so he decided to pursue a doctorate degree. He initially worked on research projects in one direction for a year before he concluded that his efforts were fruitless. He then decided to make a paradigm shift in his research direction to a new path that offered a great deal of promise with positive results, including the achievement of his doctorate degree. Nevertheless, he appeared somewhat embarrassed that it took five years beyond his BS degree to earn his doctorate degree because he contended that the norm for this accomplishment was four years. When asked what kept him going during the tough periods of failures, he replied "commitment, stick-to-itiveness, and perseverance."

On the other hand, a middle aged man shared how he was in the midst of an education doctoral degree program that he abandoned to take a job as a principal of a public high school. His chances of completing the program at a later date may be questionable.

Jamie Chamberlin highlights the ABD hurdle in an article, *Faculty offer clues to clearing the 'all-but-dissertation' hurdle.* The spirit of Chamberlin's comments is captured in the statement, "Careful planning and constructive thinking can help students avoid dissertation procrastination" (Chamberlin, 1999). Chamberlin also reported, ". . . While some students hope to get a job to help support them during their dissertation, most faculty warn against taking a faculty position or other full-time job because it can create more time conflicts."

"Being an assistant professor is hard enough already...students get caught up in the demands of the situation and they get farther and farther from their dissertation and it gets harder and harder to go back," says Jacquelynne Eccles, PhD, professor of psychology at the University of Michigan.

These personal accounts provide evidence that a *firm belief* in one's ability is critical to accomplishing the goal of completing a doctorate degree.

Time

The pursuit of the doctoral degree is a mission that requires you to fully appreciate the commitment of time required for its completion.Undertaking the doctoral degree forces you to realistically assess and balance the time span on other aspects of life such as work and/or family. Thomas B. Hoffer and Vince Welch, Jr., writing for the National Science Foundation, offer analysis on time to complete the degree, age at completion, and fields pursued over the years 1978 – 2003 (Hoffer, 2006). Hoffer and Welch give a sobering assessment of time to complete and age of hard science versus non-hard sciences degrees.

In 2003, the science and engineering fields (physical sciences, engineering, life sciences, and social sciences) had lower medians than the non-S&E broad fields (health, humanities, education, and professional/other fields) on all three time-to-degree measures. The total time-to-degree was shortest in the physical sciences (7.9 years) and longest in education (18.2 years), and the median age-at-doctorate correlated closely with the total time-to-degree measure. Doctorate recipients in the S&E fields typically earn their degrees while in their early 30s; the median for all 2003 doctorate recipients in the S&E fields was 31.8 years old. In comparison, age-at-doctorate was 34.6 years in the humanities, 37.2 years in health, 43.5 years in education, and 37.5 years in the professional/other fields category.

It is important that you have an honest assessment of the time required to complete the doctoral degree in order to set aside sufficient personal time on a daily basis for other aspects of your life such as family and work. If you are balancing a job during the pursuit of your doctoral degree, also be mindful of the use of company time and materials (e.g., company computers), which may be under scrutiny.

Financial Support

As you start to ponder Hoffer and Welch's tables, it is obvious that you need a great deal of financial support during your doctoral quest. With the economy teetering on the brink of a major recession, student loans are a causalty of the current economic crisis. Beth Healy reported for The Boston Globe on the nervousness of Bank of America to remain in the student loan business. "Bank of America Corp. yesterday said it would no longer offer private student loans, adding to the cascade of lenders pulling back in various parts of the college loan market. The bank, the third-largest student lender in the country, extended $900 million in private student loans last year. Bank of America said it would continue to offer loans that are guaranteed by the federal government, which make up 85 percent of its $6 billion student lending business" (Healy, 2008).

If your hope is to find grants, teaching assistantships and fellowships, understand that these funding sources may be available based on your degree program. John Gravois, writing in The Chronicle of Higher Education, states that:

"Between 2002 and 2006, according to data compiled by the Council of Graduate Schools, the Department of Education, the main agency supporting education research, went from giving out $41-million to graduate students to giving out $40-million. By contrast, in the same period, the National Science Foundation increased its support for graduate students working in the sciences from $153-million to $229-million, and the National Institutes of Health raised support from $651-million to $761-million for postdoctoral fellows alone." (Gravois, 2007)

Gravois offers the real nightmare of graduate students living on borrowed money. He also writes, "One spring day in 2004, during her third year of doctoral study at Howard University, Angela E. Lee received a letter from the federal government telling her she had to look elsewhere for student loans. The letter said that she had borrowed a total of $138,500 in federal student aid — a debt she had accumulated while financing her entire postsecondary education with a wearying a combination of part-time jobs, occasional assistantships, and heavy borrowing. This amount, the letter informed her, was the 'aggregate loan limit' for the government's Stafford loans. Ms. Lee was being cut off."

The most disquieting issues are what Ms. Lee heard from people outside of academia. "She remembers conversations she has had with people outside academe, who seem as baffled as they are impressed by her years of study: They say, 'Is it worth it? You're making less than me, and I only have a high-school diploma.'"

If your subgroup is overly focused on a particular degree that is not a funding priority like Education, you may have difficulty obtaining funding. African Americans may be overly represented in the Education Doctorate.The Journal of Blacks in Higher Education (JBHE) reports, "There continue to be wide differences among blacks and whites in terms of the academic fields in which they earn doctorates. For instance, 41.3 percent of all doctorates awarded to African Americans in 2004 were in the field of education. In contrast, only 19.1 percent of doctorates earned by whites were in this field. This large percentage of all African-American doctorates in the field of education has been the case for decades with only minor fluctuations." (Doctoral Degree Awards to African Americans Reach Another All-Time High, 2006)

Clearly African Americans should start to consider obtaining doctorate degrees in the areas of science, technology, engineering and mathematics (STEM). JBHE also quantified the lack of African Americans receiving STEM doctoral degrees.

"A major weakness is that blacks earned 13, or about 1 percent, of the nearly 1,200 doctorates in physics. In computer science, blacks won 0.7 percent of all Ph.D. awards. In the atmospheric sciences, less than 1 percent of all doctorates went to blacks. In chemistry, only 2.3 percent of Ph.D.s went to blacks. In the earth sciences such as geology, oceanography, and the atmospheric sciences, blacks were 1.3 percent of all doctoral recipients, down from 2.3 percent in 2003. In the ocean and marine sciences, only one of the 190 Ph.D.s in the discipline was awarded to an African American. In 2004, 148 African Americans were awarded a Ph.D. in the biological sciences. But they were only 2.5 percent of all doctorates awarded in the discipline. Black Ph.D. awards in the biological sciences did increase by 37 percent from 2003. That year, blacks were awarded 1.9 percent of all doctorates in the biological sciences."

If the funds are pouring into STEM programs and non-STEM programs are in a funding decline, one might anticipate a higher percentage of African Americans finding themselves stigmatized with the eternal ABD title. Thus, if you need grants, scholarships, fellowships, and teaching assistantships, it is incumbent that you give serious consideration to your ability to receive these opportunities with your current major.

Finally, if you are a full-time employee, your employer may underwrite the cost of your education, assuming they see your degree as an asset to the corporation or social agency.

Doctoral Peer

Although many people are very proud of their masters' degrees, there is a significant mindset metamorphosis necessary to evolve from the dutiful modus operandi of masters' and bachelors' degrees to leadership modus vivendi expected at the doctoral degree level. Graduate students enchanted by traits of professorial appeasement or gofer-ism may find little respect in the eyes of their doctoral advisor or doctoral committee members.

I was meeting with a corporate technical manager at a company located in the Ozarks in the early 1990s when a young engineer brought some data to the manager. When the manager looked at the data he became very stressed at what the young engineer had provided. I was initially puzzled at the manager's displeasure. He recognized my concern, so he said that the young engineer had done no more than what he would expect from a technician. The technical manager went on stating that it was the young engineer's responsibility to interpret the data. The managerial disconnect was that the technical manager was looking for the young engineer to demonstrate leadership potential to be able to handle tomorrow's technical investigations. On the other hand, the young engineer apparently viewed himself as a gofer.

In a chat with a gentleman estimated to be in his middle forties, I heard disquieting tales of his journey to a doctoral degree where being a good gofer worked against his progress. He worked an entire summer collecting data for his research advisor, who was off on a foreign trip. When the research advisor returned, this doctoral student learned that the data was useless; therefore, it was discarded. What is troubling in this story is that the doctoral student had travelled 160 miles twice per week to collect this bad data.

This doctoral student added another disconcerting tale to demonstrate his advisor's abuse. As he started to speak, his facial expression became eerie to the point where my wife and I felt a sense of discomfort with the discussion. He conjured up a deeply hidden, passionate disdain for his advisor who he believed was an academic tyrant. This distraught gentleman said that he then decided to take a needed course at a different campus of the university that was 80 miles away. When his advisor returned from his summer trip, the doctoral student was told that although he took the same course at a different campus of the university, it was unsatisfactory. Therefore, the doctoral student was required to retake the same course under his advisor for it to qualify towards his doctoral degree. The doctoral student was beaten down by the professor, but retook the course. By now this gentleman was extremely emotionally disturbed during the discussion, to the point that he was breathing hard and became restless, since he was recalling a dark period in his life. My eyes were glued in his direction as it was clear he was recounting all of his bitterness experienced with the whole doctoral degree effort. Despite these setbacks, he persevered and earned the doctoral degree. His wife chimed in to say that she had a Master's degree and her husband's awful experience had dissuaded her from pursuing a doctorate degree.

The other side of this story is when a doctoral student demonstrates leadership suggesting that he or she possesses the right qualities to be a doctoral peer. A lady estimated to be in her early fifties shared how her advisor at a major university attempted to rattle her determination in pursuing the doctoral degree. When she brought a draft of her dissertation to her advisor, the advisor merely dropped the paper in a trash can in front of her. She was devastated at her advisor's antic, but did not allow this incident to take her mind off of her objective to get a doctorate degree. She swallowed her pride, and reached into the trash to recover the dissertation. She reworked it and offered the upgraded version to her advisor, demonstrating her stern determination. Once it was clear that this doctoral candidate had passed the advisor's litmus test on fortitude, the two ladies became friends. Yet this doctoral candidate recalled this trying tale with some disdain in her voice. After the doctoral candidate earned the doctoral degree she went on to become a dean at a university.

Academic Tenacity

A Catholic nun shared that she had an inadequate undergraduate preparation for graduate school. Her undergraduate degree program did not include mathematics requirements, and she found herself in the midst of a doctoral program that required her to take statistics courses. This forced her to attempt to pass mathematics graduates courses based on her high school mathematics background. I asked the nun how she managed her stresses in such a difficult situation, to which she replied that she had advisors with whom she could talk in moments of high stress, and that she also prayed a lot.

A second academic challenge for the nun came when she was ready to defend her doctoral dissertation. There was a member of her doctoral committee who was aware of her shortcomings in statistics. This member appeared determine on making the nun's dissertation defense turn into a nerve-racking event until the committee chairman stepped in and stopped the academic power play

Today, the nun is one of the head nuns in an order of nuns.

Jamie Chamberlin offers some guidance in these types of situations. "Start early. Be honest with yourself. Prepare a budget. If necessary, apply for financial aid. Avoid internships . . . Pick the right help. Keep a narrow focus. Accept the criticism. Prepare in advance for the oral defense. Keep cool."

The key lesson the nun's story offers is that when things look academically impossible, they may actually be possible if you do not give up. The nun could have complained, "Woe is me," but instead she recognized her deficiency and developed an effort to compensate for her mathematics shortfall.

I personally learned this lesson in academic tenacity when I worked midnight to 8:00 a.m. at a plant and initially had to hitchhike 100 miles round trip to go to college where I was majoring in mathematics. A few old men noticed my efforts to get to college from the plant, and started to stop by my house at 10:00 p.m. to drive me to the plant. The next morning I would hitchhike the 40 remaining miles to the college and back 50 miles after classes. Another old man that lived about 15 miles from the college decided to take me to his turn-off point, from which I hitchhiked the remainder of the distance. When I got home my studying came first, so I usually got only a few hours of rest because I was hoping my youth would allow me to withstand the high stresses associated with my degree quest.

One day my wife came by on an interstate transport bus and saw me hitchhiking in the snow. When I got home that night she laid her head onto my chest and she started to cry. She asked, "Why do you do it?" My response was, "Because I believe that each day I am on that road is one more step towards my goal." The next year we moved to Dover, the home of Delaware State University (DSU), and I got a car. I graduated from DSU with a degree in mathematics and almost enough credits in physics to also receive a degree in physics.

Academic Servitude

The senior citizen chemist mentioned above also shared the story of another degree candidate who took 11 years to complete his

PhD. The PhD advisor's exploitation was the explanation for this extraordinarily long doctoral degree pursuit. According to the senior citizen, the graduate student was an excellent researcher whose doctoral advisor did not want to let him go. A definitive answer was not provided from the senior citizen chemist when asked why the research advisor finally let the graduate student go, but he intimated that the doctoral student was viewed as being in academic bondage and that appearance of academic exploitation contradicted the university's public image.

A social scientist in his early sixties also shared an account of being trapped in an endless cycle of being asked to supply new data on research efforts by his research advisor at a major university, which he perceived as academic exploitation. His frustration with academic exploitation forced him to conclude that he was on a senseless doctoral quest at his present university and to abandon this particular university. Nevertheless, he still had a very strong interest in obtaining the doctoral degree and decided that a change of venue was the right decision, although he took the chance of losing many graduate credits in the process. This social scientist completed a doctoral degree in education at a new university.

In this case, the caution here is for the doctoral graduate student not to allow all his or her attention to be focused on meeting the needs of the research advisor while ignoring his or her own progress towards the doctoral degree. It becomes incumbent for the doctoral candidate not to appear as the dutiful gofer who is afraid to challenge his or her advisor over the inability to make academic progress under the advisor's tutelage. The danger of the doctoral student becoming enchanted with playing the role of the dutiful gofer is that it may suggest that they may not be perceived as a doctoral peer. As long the doctoral student does not complain, the advisor may continue to exploit this situation.

Ogden sees getting the doctoral degree as a rite of passage. ". . .You have to be able to convince your advisors that your goals, objectives, and abilities are congruent enough with theirs so that they are willing to consider you a colleague. The 'passage' is from, me student—you professors to 'us colleagues.' The rites are all the things you do to signal the professors that you have entered upon the passage and, finally, with a successful oral defense of your dissertation, have completed the journey."

Doctoral Committee Politics

One of my outside committee members cautioned me on the importance of having committee members who work well together. He pointed out that a nightmarish situation occurs when two committee members dislike each other and you become the instrument they employ to put down each other's efforts. I am thankful that my doctoral committee members worked well together, so I wasted no time stressing over political gamesmanship between committee members.

Chamberlin offers comments that doctoral students should take to heart. "When assembling the committee, it's important for students to select faculty that work well together, says Eccles. Students' committee meetings can become a battleground for departmental politics if they don't first investigate possible faculty conflict."

However, this assumes you can select your committee.

"The interplay between committee members can occasionally be horrendous," agrees Stuart Tentoni, PhD, health center counseling coordinator and clinical professor of educational psychology at the University of Wisconsin - Milwaukee. 'Some committee members are in the room only to prove to each other why they are there—often at the expense of the student.'"

A doctoral committee chairman possessing political clout can prevent difficult situations materializing before a thesis or dissertation defense takes place. A scientist shared that as a first year doctoral student he made the mistake of correcting an error in a report of a professor who did not appreciate a lowly graduate student highlighting his shortcoming. This scientist was stressed since he knew that this professor could sabotage his doctoral defense. However, his research advisor also was the department chairman, who made it clear to the potentially vindictive professor that he could expect his own students to experience a difficult time passing their dissertation defense should he harass the young scientist. The scientist said this political move by his advisor allowed him to pass through the dissertation defense without any complications.

On the other hand, having a laissez faire committee chairman can be equally disasterous. A fellow who received his doctoral degree in the United Kingdom said it was generally understood during his tenure in graduate school for mathematics that most people graduated. He was groomed for the doctoral degree in high school, and during his undergraduate years his focus was mainly on mathematics courses, for it was not necessary to take liberal arts courses. The doctoral program had high level courses names of which few people had heard. However, one of his fellow graduate students had a committee chairman who paid little attention to his work. When this hapless doctoral student went to present and defend his dissertation, he failed and left the university with the consolation prize of the Masters of Philosophy that carried the stigma of academic failure.

Chapter II

The Writer's Mindset

In the first step of our journey in learning to write theses, reports and papers quickly, we use the model of the new writer trying to overcome writer's block as a guide to conquering our own procrastination. We shall view thesis and dissertation writing as no more difficult than other writing forms. Through the eyes of a writer overwhelmed by writer's obstacles, we will glean some ideas on how social and hard science doctoral students can overcome writing gridlock.

Imagine getting up Saturday morning, dashing out of your house and hopping into your car for a spin. The next thing you know you are zipping down the expressway without a care in the world, enchanted by beautiful music filling your ears. Being a task-oriented person, roughly a half hour later you ask yourself, "Where am I going? Gas costs roughly two dollars a gallon, so am I just wasting money driving in circles?"

You abhor wasting time and money. The first thought that pops into your mind is, "Do I turn around?" This is followed by another disquieting question, "Do I pull off the road until I can really decide what to do?" Before your nerves calm down, you are whispering to yourself, "I'll wait for a divine revelation, and then I'll know what to do."

Your previous joy is now a headache because turning around means you have wasted time, money for gasoline, and the wear and tear on your automobile. James Wilmore, former Fire Chief of the City of Wilmington, Delaware, has a saying that describes your decision-making dilemma. "You get nothing for starting and stopping."

Your stress heightens as you realize the foolhardiness in continuing to drive aimlessly for it means that you are going nowhere fast. You are a person who likes to control his or her own destiny thus, you are perturbed that your well-being is now in the hands of fate. Instinctively, you know that counting on luck is only for professional gamblers. Ordinary people are discomfited by the idea of "luck."

Having writer's block is like driving a car without a travel plan. Picture a person staring into a huge, blank computer screen with bloodshot eyes, fingers locked in a writing position: writer's block! Yet this nightmare and Herculean task need not become self-defeating if you get your mind set in the proper order for writing. Using the driving scenario, let us develop the proper mindset for writing your thesis or dissertation, internal corporate reports and publishable papers that are user-friendly.

We hear many excuses for people not writing reports and articles. An industrial research scientist provided a classic: "Trade journal articles are a real labor of love." You hear phrases like, "I love to write literature but not that boring technical stuff." Still others contend, "That literary stuff is just too emotional for me to waste my time on. I need to get to the point and not waste a lot of time describing the sky as blue and the trees green."

Pulling off the road to plan your journey is comparable to my first basic principle of good writing:

1. Have a clear mind to capture your emotions, because pens, pencils, word processors, and typewriters are mere tools for putting your thoughts into words.

In learning to write newspaper articles, I rewrote my first effort eleven times before something of publishing caliber emerged. Asked to look at the first draft, my wife Gwynelle commented, "It is the worst thing I have ever read."

Her words were a crushing blow to my ego and engendered an "I'll show you" attitude. But in the final analysis Gwynelle was right. My draft lacked coherent thinking and merely rambled over some vague issue.

Driven solely by pride to regain my stature in Gwynelle's eyes, I rewrote the article again and again repeating, however, the same mistakes. After nine rewrites my nerves calmed and my mind opened. It was clear that I needed to think before attempting to write, so a five-mile walk seemed the perfect thing to do. During this walk my thoughts became clear, and I could see the issue as plain as day. Once it was clear what I was going to write about, it took only two drafts to get something publishable: one draft to record my emotion and another draft to clean up the grammar. I was later paid for this work.

This learning experience guided my writing on my master's and doctoral theses, over 600 newspaper editorials, letters-to-editor, technical, trade and business reports, presentations and articles, and several books during my career to date. It made me prolific enough to write seven internal technical reports, three technical articles and presentations for business societies, and roughly thirty newspaper editorials in 1993, the year I retired from the DuPont Company as a Technical Marketing Specialist. Thus, my varied writing experiences have taught me that the basis of quick writing is,

2. Five minutes of thinking is worth five hours of writing.

No one is surprised to hear research scientists and engineers say, "Just give me the data and I'm happy, but don't ask me to write it up. It takes me forever to get something written," or social science students say, "I can pass the courses, but I am worried about writing the doctoral thesis." These statements can mean career suicide for some corporate and university scientists and engineers because they are in a "publish or perish" job when it comes to upward mobility. It can mean the social science major gets tagged with the initialism ABD for infinity.

If technocrats or social scientists think clearly about the one emotion they want their intended audience to take from their thesis or dissertation, article, report, or presentation, they will not find writing an overwhelming experience. Remember that writing with non-clarified ideas is like asking your audience to build a puzzle without any idea of the shape of the pieces or their color scheme. Don't be intimidated by a blank computer screen begging your fingers to do something.

> 3. *Forethought can mentally write the first, second, and third draft* of your work, placing you on the path to producing an excellent publication or a very convincing story in short order.

Forethought is sometimes discarded with the excuse that "I know what I want to say, but I just can't seem to say it." A closer look at this comment suggests that we really don't know what we want to say, and have refused to ponder the subject long enough to arrive at what needs to be presented. Or we are nervous that others will exploit our efforts against us. We may not have considered to whom the work is directed. We may not be sure of our overt and covert agendas in doing this work. We may be afraid to write up our technical work for it will highlight the holes in our research.

> 4. *A good vision statement is a key element in rapid writing* for theses or dissertations, technical and newspaper articles, newsletters, and books.

This statement gives meaning to your work by providing you with a holistic assessment of your data that permits you to produce a consistent story that the audience can understand. It is also necessary if you want your work to be user-friendly, for it reduces the writing fog factor by focusing on writing an understandable document. On the other hand, you must write to the academic level expected in your profession. However, people contemplating careers in the public or private sector may find it is better to have mainstream understanding of your work, for you significantly enhance the chances of it being used and of you being rewarded.

Vision statements address key issues: will your thesis or dissertation, article or book make obsolete an existing theory? Are you telling your peers that you have developed an improved or new product, or clarified scientific understanding, or observed some new trend in social activity? Do you want to merely show off your expertise in a given area?

Establishing your vision statement and clarifying issues is the business of your first mental draft. This activity is critical to further writing efforts. Not doing this job well will lead to many frustrating moments and difficulty in writing. The danger is that you do not fully comprehend what your advisor is requesting and you generate data that is useless, as was the case in the story above where the doctoral student spent a full summer collecting the wrong data. Or the scope of your task is too broad, making it unlikely that you will accomplish your mission. If there is any doubt in your mind on what your advisor wishes you to achieve, it is advisable to request your charge to be put in writing and for you to discuss this letter with them until all doubt is gone.

In writing the second mental draft, you want to begin to answer the questions posed in the vision statement of your first draft. Here is where you must separate fact from fantasy. Trying to do too much in one report will make it very confusing and difficult to write. Therefore, if you have multiple issues in your vision statement, perhaps you should rethink it. A good vision statement is nothing more than a holistic idea of what you want the outcome of your report to be. It is usually best if one single unifying thought makes up this statement.

> *5. What are the core findings of my work,* and how do I wish to present them to the doctoral committee or senior public or private management? Do I have access to the data I need to make my case? Did my data come from credible sources and sound research?

In your third mental draft, start addressing tactical issues that get the writing process underway, such as the series of questions above that need mental answers to stimulate your writing.

You also start to overlay your vision with the amount of resources you have to make the final result a reality. This can be a arduous process, because an honest assessment of your thesis or dissertation's publishing potential (for both your university departmental staff, your public or private sector employer's staff and for outside publications that can evolve from this work) is a necessary condition for expending your time on it. You must ask yourself, "Does my intended audience really care what I have to say, and if they do, what piques their interest?"

If you get trapped in the chasm between fact and fantasy, you will find out that the doctoral committee and publishing houses have no problem letting you know that your work does not meet their idea of publishable research. You might find yourself in the situation of the British graduate student as reported above, who failed the dissertation defense.

6. *Once your self-analysis is done, you are in a strong position* to place your efforts before your doctoral committee or management, if that becomes necessary.

You are now ready to write mental draft number four. The cost of obtaining credible data now stares you in the face if you do not already have it. If you conclude that the cost is too great for the benefit, you should terminate your plans before you waste valuable time and money. Management has a limited budget from which to operate, and a strong case gives you an advantage in getting their support for your project.

The fourth mental draft also gives you an opportunity to re-ask, "Who really is my audience? What data do I really need to make my case? *Can I write my vision statement down in three sentences or less (preferably one sentence)? If the answer is no, you need to restart the writing process.*

A clear vision statement is the cornerstone of rapid writing and its refinement gets you through the first four drafts of your work. Time spent perfecting your vision statement will pay large dividends in making your writing work successful.

Chapter III

Key Report Elements

When you are attempting to write your doctoral thesis or dissertation quickly, a presupposition is that you have a crystal clear picture in your mind of what you intend to say. If you have any doubts, you may find yourself caught in the quagmire of writer's block.

Doubt is a productivity encumbrance, for you are struggling to discern what data is important to tell your story at a level of doctoral competence, so you may spend many hours hoarding and stressing over insignificant data. You do not want to pad your research paper with nonsensical material because you have not clearly thought out what you intend to say. It may become tempting to commit the mortal sin of thinking, "I didn't really have anything substantive to say, so I will dazzle them with balderdash." You must remember that your doctoral committee members are all experts in their own right, so it's foolish on your part to attempt to underestimate their capabilities. You also should keep in mind that your thesis is not the place for demonstrating your creative writing talents unless you are writing works based on demonstrating creative writing skills. A comment from an old television show is apropos here, "Just the facts!"

Additionally, there are four key writer's tools you need to have to write your doctoral thesis: a clear *vision statement*, a set of *premises*, the *test measurements or theoretical calculations*, and a *computer*.

A detailed discussion of each of the four key writer's tools will follow; however, we want to give some working definitions of terms involved in the coming discussion to maintain clarity:

Vision statement is the picture in your mind of the outcome on your audience from reading your thesis.

Premises are the ground rules to viewing your data when it comes time to analyze it. They are things you assume to be true, although you may find later from your data that they need refining or are simply not true and must be discarded.

Data are the experimental measurements or theoretical calculations that fuel the thesis. Whenever you record information you should add a brief analysis to reduce confusion later as to what it really means. You felt some justification for collecting the information, so the collection time may be the best time to write down your rationale. A research notebook is an excellent way to keep data combined with an analysis of it that can be retrieved easily. I personally found writing research progress reports to the Dean of Arts and Science during my teaching tenure at Delaware State University on my efforts to improve pass rates in business calculus helped me to cull the data collected before attempting to write a doctoral thesis at the University of Delaware.

A computer is the personal computer, workstation, or mainframe terminal that offers word processing, graphics, spreadsheet, database and access to the Internet. Although some people may want to write things out in longhand, it is incumbent that you learn to type your ideas in an electronic format that will make them accessible to other people throughout the world who may have significant upgrades to your research effort. You also ought to learn to use search engines such as Google, Yahoo, Ask, Bing, and so on to make literatures searches outside of the library on works that others have done in your area of reporting.

The computer should have software installed at least of the 2003 basic Microsoft Office level word processing, spreadsheet, and graphic software capability. You may find that your university may require you to use Microsoft Office so that the documents you generate are compatible with others at your institution. In writing your thesis you may find Microsoft Word's tracking feature allows your doctoral committee members to comment on an electronic version of your thesis, so you have a clear guide as to what upgrades you must make. Furthermore, you should have the capability to make a PDF file directly from your application that can permit it to be printed out across various computer operating systems.

These four writing tools (see Figure 3.1) are the means to developing your doctoral thesis or technical report. The importance of having each item cannot be overemphasized, as they will assist you in avoiding getting bogged down in a quagmire of confusion.

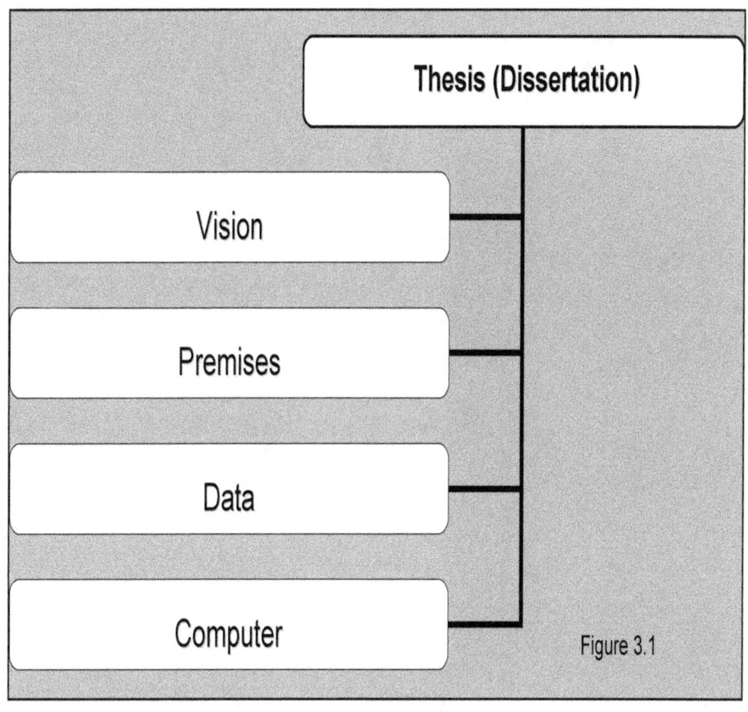

Figure 3.1

Chapter IV

Thesis Writing Elements

You are now ready to employ a report writing template to get the writing effort underway. I offer generalized technical report elements with the underpinning thought that your final report can readily evolve into a thesis. Figure 4.1 gives the generalized report writing elements (Miller, The Quick White Paper, 1999) as a prototypical writing template. The full writing template is found in the Appendix (Research and Technical Report Writing Template).

The ability to write several reports simultaneously using this Research and Technical Report Writing Template hinges on clearly writing each of the below elements in such a way that they are portable to new instruments, and that all tables, charts and graphs have conclusions written on them whenever appropriate.

Report Writing Elements

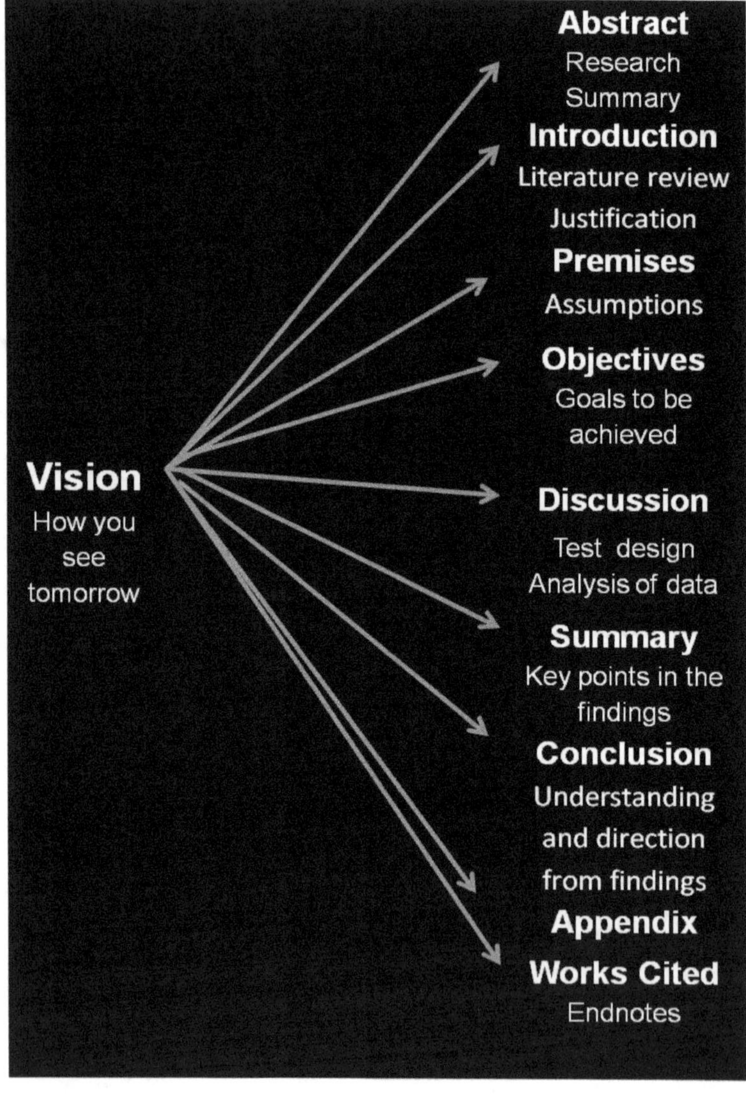

Figure 4.1

Tables

In writing a thesis, you may wish to exclude table conclusions to meet the requirements that your university specifies in their thesis and dissertation guidelines. However, if you include conclusions in your tables, it reduces problems with analyzing large amounts of data later. Table 4.1 offers an example of a table with conclusions.

Filament Analysis

Kink Bands: Heavy = 500+ Medium = 250+ Light= 100-

Very Light= 25- Very Very Light= 5-

Sample	#	Kink Bands	Fibrillation	Split	Crushed Ends
	1	390	20	0	4
	2	250	20	1	6
	3	178	21	1	2
	4	255	20	0	2
	5	112	21	0	1

* High fibrillation suggests cord abrasion
* Crushed ends reduce cord strength

Table 4.1

We also need to look closer at charts, graphs, and tables with an eye towards data portability, because data collected in papers written during the time you took the required doctoral level courses may be very useable in the doctoral thesis or dissertation. Table 4.1 contains a principal rating system for the key data displayed, namely kink bands. It includes summaries of several observations, and ends with conclusions stating what the data indicates. These details allow the author to easily turn Table 4.1 into a PowerPoint presentation to be given in a seminar or to a technical society.

On the other hand, Table 4.2 is designed for an audience with sufficient technical expertise to readily appreciate the findings. Test scores below are taken from a doctoral thesis for an education doctorate degree. This data would be appreciated by a cross section of education researchers and practitioners.

Fall 1998 First Test Scores

	Finite Math	Business Calculus
Mean	41.82	48.57
Standard Deviation	22.24	18.41
Numbers Students	22	30

Table 4.2

Charts

Continuing this portability discussion, we now turn to charts. There are basically two types. The first family of charts are those that help you to understand the science of an issue; they do not lend themselves to having conclusions written on them. The second family of charts are those with conclusions to your research.

Figure 4.3 helps to paint a clear picture of the parameters of low-twist versus high-twist yarn and cord for hose manufacturers. It reduces the complexity of points you are making to diverse groups. Figure 4.3 first appeared in the technical paper entitled, "Knitted Heater Hose Static Equations: Burst Pressure and Economics," presented at the International Society of Industrial Fabric Manufacturers Fall Conference in 1993.

HELIX ANGLE

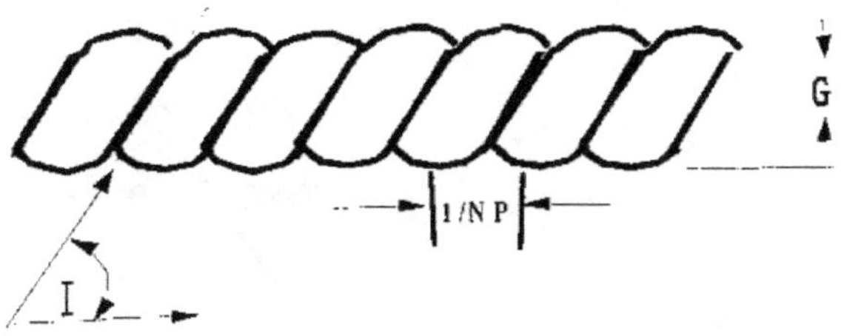

N = Turns/Inch P = Number of Plies

G = Cord Gauge (Mils)

I = Helix Angle

Figure 4.3

Figure 4.4 is a comparable chart to Figure 4.3, only it is being directed to an audience of educators. It shows that the course is being taught on an exponential curve where students' background deficiencies are addressed in the initial section of the semester. This chart contains very little detail since its goal is to convey a teaching style.

Figures 4.3 and 4.4 convey information at a glance. These charts offer persons who are not fluent in the language of the thesis a feel for what you are suggesting. This family of figures can explain concepts that are difficult to write up by using a picture.

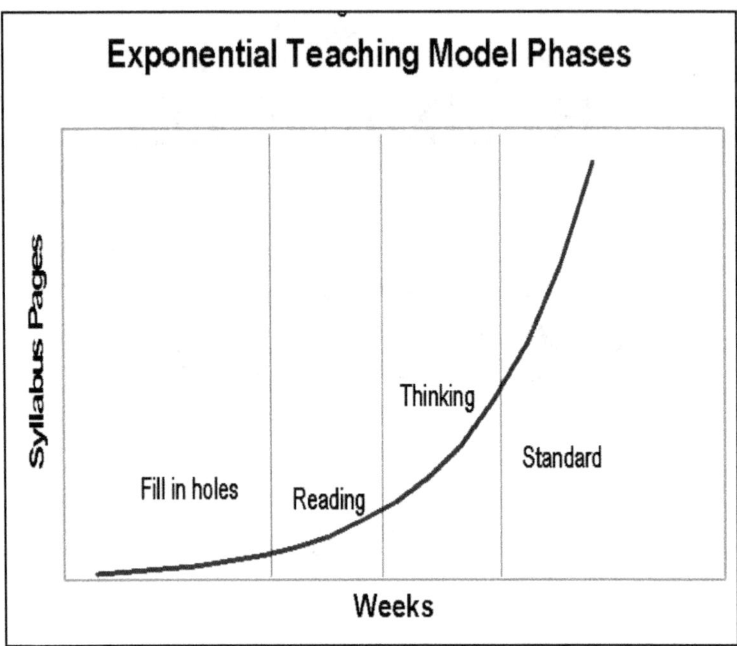

Figure 4.4

Usages of the Report Writing Elements

You now are pondering writing your doctoral thesis once you have developed your vision statement. You are ready once again to take inventory of interim reports stored on your computer to pull together your paper. You discover how simple it is to merely extract a portion of your master report to meet an immediate need; especially when you are pressed to produce new reports quickly. The thesis becomes less daunting when you have a significant portion already done, perhaps in the first papers you wrote when you started your doctoral journey. It is usually a lot easier to do some mild editing or create paragraphs from one-line statements written yesterday than to start anew each time you are going to create a thesis, book, or journal publication.

If you make the extra effort to write your doctoral research papers, many variations can evolve from them to target a host of audiences. This generation of new reports merely becomes a withdrawal from your reports' storehouse, dependent upon how well you learned to use word processing, spreadsheet, and graphic programs.

What I am suggesting is that you start writing your doctoral thesis with the first paper you turn in to be graded in graduate school. The ability to write the doctoral thesis quickly is straight forward when you develop a vision statement, write the first four drafts in your mind, check the data that you have in inventory to see if it is sufficient to answer many of the questions under debate, and take new data to address issues that have not been addressed.

Chapter V

Writing Elements Defined

We are now ready to start the actual thesis-writing effort. We will take the issues we discussed thus far and quickly create reports that the university advisor will find thesis-or dissertation-caliber material. Earlier we established the elements of a report-writing template that possesses the power to generate papers in a timely manner, but we never defined these elements in a way useful to social and hard scientists and engineers. Since a picture is often worth a thousand words, the Report Writings Elements (Figure 4.1) model above contains the key elements for developing a comprehensive report. It encompasses the needs of many university research paper writing projects including the doctoral thesis.

We will examine each element by defining it and, where appropriate, will offer actual examples from published papers or a doctoral thesis. Our efforts will focus on your learning to use the report-writing template as the master guide to generate a high caliber research report that has portable elements. With such, you can freely extract whatever elements necessary to generate other reports or presentations that address specific requests from your research advisor.

Vision Statement

What do we mean by vision?

Vision, simply put, is the mental picture of how you want your report or thesis to be received when it is read by your target audience. Perhaps you visualize your report being embraced by your research advisor or peers, so that your research credibility is enhanced by your unique findings. You might highlight in a study that your local school district is wasting money trying to use "Some canned instruction effort" versus allowing the teachers to use their own creativity in the classroom.

I was visiting a dean and observed an advanced age doctoral candidate share his vision for the dissertation that he was hoping to write for another university. It was quite clear that the dean was spending significant effort trying to help this doctoral candidate to settle on a vision that would generate a doable project. He was attempting a grandiose effort that required the collection of a large amount of data, the collection of which was proving diffult. There was the concern that he was attempting to solve an undefined problem. This scenario suggests that this doctoral candidate is much like the earlier scenario of a person getting into his or her car and driving for hours without a clue as to where he or she is going, and wasting time and money to accomplish nothing. This scenario is troubling because this doctoral candidate has the potential of becoming an eternal ABD if he gets overwhelmed in the minutiae of data. The key message is that the vision statement must be a doable project that could iterate into a much larger program with time.

If your goal is to complete your business report, doctoral thesis, or other report quickly, then attempting to write without first establishing a clear vision statement is tantamount to walking into several shopping malls merely to look at the merchandise, in the hope that sudden inspiration will suggest what you should buy. On the other hand, if you need a new pair of shoes, you know to focus your visit on shoe stores. You may ignore other stores. There is no doubt that wasted time at the mall is kept to a minimum.

It is safe to say that the time spent developing your vision statement will be paid back tenfold in reduced frustration when it comes time to write your doctoral thesis.

A good vision statement is the linchpin in writing high-caliber reports and theses in a timely manner. Vision is simply how you want things to be tomorrow after your audience has read your work today.

Abstract

Scientific and nonscientific papers usually start with an abstract (that may be a paragraph or more) that is meant to encourage the reader to read the paper by providing a capsule summary of the work. When librarians do a literature search on a particular subject, they supply the abstract to researchers, who rely upon it to decide if the article or report is pertinent to their effort. On the other hand, many researchers will do online searches and use the library to get documents that they cannot access on the Internet. This suggests that your abstract must be very informative on the findings reported in your thesis or dissertation.

There are three key elements in an abstract that make it a good tool for assessing the importance of your research effort. It should offer a *rationale* for why you did the work, list the *tests* performed, and provide the scientific *results* from your effort.

Rationale

Academia has the responsibility to be on the forefront of knowledge where the public good becomes the driving force for their research effort. This suggests that universities need to share with the general public their findings in a manner that shows that tax dollars are being put to a productive use. Universities may also need to provide private foundations with assurance that they are researching the issues which they agreed to study when research grants were bestowed. The first statement in the abstract should center on a rationale for your research.

> In the late 1990s, the failure rate of business students at [a middle level university] in both finite mathematics and business calculus courses reached an estimated 50 percent. In response, students were given blackboard assignments and an algebra placement examination to establish the classes' academic preparation for handling both finite mathematics and business calculus courses. During blackboard assignments, students were required to write out the instructions and problems before attempting to develop answers. It became apparent that significant textbook-reading deficiencies existed in both courses. The algebra placement examination highlighted a significant background deficiency in fundamental algebraic concept knowledge. These academic background deficiencies in reading and algebra suggested that direct instruction may have needed augmentation to meet the needs of a background-deficient population. A teaching research effort was undertaken to find teaching variants on direct instruction or to propose alternative teaching methods to help background deficient populations become successful in finite mathematics and business calculus courses.

Test Program

If you ran tests, you should state the nature of them. You may consider statements such as, "Used photo micrographic studies of nylon filaments to study bundle shapes after exposure to a lateral axis crushing force of 10 Newtons per square millimeter."

In this statement you are telling the reader that you examined the filaments under a microscope to look for damage, and you took pictures of what you observed. This tells the reader to expect pictures that show your findings.

However, in cases where your work is a theoretical treatise, you will want to highlight your ability to calculate different variables without the need to use valuable resources to produce test items. For instance, the following statement may be considered for social science:

> The lecture teaching style was assessed, and it was learned that lecturing should stay under 50 percent of the class period for both finite mathematics and business calculus. Classroom activities should occupy the remainder of time

to avoid problems with students maintaining their attentiveness. The material coverage in the courses following an exponential teaching model was assessed where the initial portion of the semester focused on filling in background deficiencies, and in the later portion there was an accelerating material coverage pace. Experiments in dropping test scores on one test to evaluate the impact on student dropout rates suggested only the first or second test should be dropped, to avoid good students becoming mediocre performers when they realize they have earned an "A." Some good students may fail to master the higher-level material in the course if they lose their focus in the latter portion of the semester. Course dropout rates ran roughly 10 percent. The use of direct instruction was found to be satisfactory for teaching finite mathematics when used along with three teaching supplements: the Modified Bragg Grading System, the Exponential Teaching model, and a capstone project.

Results

The results are the ultimate justification of your work, for they tell your research advisor that you responded to a need. You either accomplished their mission or their goal was beyond the scope of present technology. Thus, doctoral committees will look for definitive conclusions and should not get a sense that you are waffling, for that would suggest that your findings are suspect.

You might write a results statement as follows:

Found radial cracks and a permanent bundle deformation that reduced the normal force component in the frictional force used to retain the hose fitting.

In this statement you have told the reader that in textile hose reinforcements the fitting is held on by frictional force, and the normal force component necessary for producing this force is changing. This should pique the reader's interest to want to know if such things as time and temperature are important here.

An example of a hard science abstract is,

"Hose manufacturers constantly seek better techniques for assessing their hose economics. They are also using more and more textile reinforcements to produce hoses to meet demanding applications in automotive and industrial markets. Thus, hose manufacturers need a set of equations that permits them to do paper studies on textile hose designs to avoid the costly process of making each item. Equations, derived from empirical data on PPD-T Aramid, nylon, polyester, and MPD-T Aramid for knitted hose economies are offered. There are also equations offered to estimate the cord gauge that is a necessary input for calculating inner-liner coverage in knit, spiral, and braided hoses. Having a good estimate of the cord gauge is very important in obtaining good hose burst pressure because low inner-liner pack leads to pinhole failures. On the other hand, excessive pack can cause delamination without secondary adhesion systems present."

Since the social science abstract may be longer, I will only give a portion of my doctoral thesis abstract to avoid repeating the information already shared.

"In an assessment of direct instruction with background deficient business calculus students, it was concluded that the significant algebra background need was too high to port the finite mathematics-teaching model over to business calculus. Students were put into teams to work on class assignments where the teacher selected which team member would present the team's work on the blackboard to insure individual accountability. Teams anchored with academically strong students proved to work well with business calculus coupled with the exponential teaching model and the Modified Bragg Grading system.

Employing the Wulff misalignment model of the student's mathematical background deficiencies, course content, and teacher teaching style offers a framework for insight into some future actions that [the university] may want to take. Recommendations are offered, including:

• hiring a faculty teaching consultant,

• developing workshops on the cooperative learning style of teaching,

- expanding the registration system to control students taking courses without necessary prerequisites,

- giving instructors a copy of student course-taking history,

- offering teaching consultancy to instructors with high student failure rates,

- granting tenure based on teaching excellence,

- apprising students of consequences for course dropping decisions,

- suggesting to teachers the need to teach reading, and

- empowering instructors to drop students for non-attendance in class.

A detailed discussion of the improvement effort covering both finite mathematics and business calculus is in Appendix C, 'Demystifying Business Calculus: Teaching with a Practical Business Mindset.' A key achievement in this improvement effort is to encourage both finite mathematics and business calculus students to pursue academic excellence instead of exploiting a 'just passing' strategy.

In writing your doctoral thesis or dissertation, you must be mindful of data that cannot be given out to the general public because it was shared with you in confidence. You have to protect the names of your interviewees if they demand anonymity. As a national columnist, I have found that if people know you will keep their confidence, they will share a great deal of confidential information that will often direct your efforts in finding key information in the public domain. I follow the adage, "When in doubt, leave it out!" You ought to keep in mind that second-guessing whether or not to use some information given to you in secrecy that may cause you or someone else public embarrassment can significantly delay your ability to write. The bottom line is to avoid unnecessary stressors when attempting to write your thesis or dissertation.

Introduction

In the introduction you survey the literature, pointing out what has been done in the past and how your work contributes to new learning. This avoids your coming out with a me-too article that will only put your audience to sleep because it offers nothing novel.

Often, completing a search of the current literature requires that you work closely with a librarian, for references are not always easy to locate. Sometimes you find that there are articles that need translating. A historical approach, giving excerpts from a series of articles that lead up to your present work, is a straightforward way of writing an introduction. You are simply placing things in chronological order, thereby highlighting a chasm in the literature that you intend to fill. The introduction should be of sufficient length to bring out the key articles that offer credibility to your research effort.

Below is a portion of the introduction from my doctoral thesis that was written to be a standalone book.

> In fall 1998, DSU changed the mathematics course sequence for business majors to college algebra, finite mathematics, business calculus, and statistics.
>
> In 2000, I left the Wilmington campus to teach on the Main Delaware State University campus in Dover, DE, where the student population was overwhelmingly traditional students. Still School of Management (SOM) students were having significant problems passing the new required mathematics courses to qualify for SOM bachelor degree programs. The mathematics department chairperson estimated that the mathematics failure rate was fifty percent for SOM students in mathematics courses (2000 personal conversation with Hanson Umoh). When I joined, the Dean of Arts and Science requested that I help to develop teaching techniques to ameliorate this academic crisis. It was apparent that there needed to be a cultural change. A focus on the business students' success needed to become the new mantra with the new curriculum. Nevertheless, I hoped to kindle subtly an economic awakening to the long-term potential deleterious impact on the University of ignoring this needed paradigm shift in thinking on teaching mathematics.

Since the mathematics curriculum change did not resolve the high failure rate problem of the SOM students, the SOM and mathematics department interdepartmental tension remained. Daniel Goleman, Richard Boyatzis, and Annie McKee offer a disquieting comment that could have portended the long-term fallout of the above interdepartmental chasm on the mathematics instructors' teaching enthusiasm with business students. 'Once defensiveness sets in, it typically demotivates rather than motivates, thereby interrupting, even stopping self-directed learning and the likelihood of change.' (Goleman, et. al., p. 137).

In an effort to start bridging this chasm, I needed to work with everyone from an emotional level to foster change. Goleman, et. al., offers a comment that could have been a template for my emotions at the start of this teaching research effort. 'When a leader focuses on people, emotional bonds are created that are the ground in which resonance is sown—and people will follow that leader in good times and bad. Resonance creates an invisible but powerful bond between people based on a belief in what they are doing and a belief in one another' (Goleman, et, al., p. 221).

It would be easy to look at this interdepartmental friction as solely between two schools in a university, but that would miss the real significance of what was happening. Furthermore, any solutions proposed might only address a symptom. A discussion with a military officer on the time required in producing Reserve Officer Candidates on today's college campuses offered a holistic look at the DSU interdepartmental tension problem. She made the case that the military did not understand it requiring more than four years for an ROTC candidate to graduate from college. Her comments corroborated the DaimlerChrysler management desires, thus suggesting a refocus of the research approach from the DSU schism to one where improved graduation potential was the real goal. Since one might expect business faculty and students to be very pragmatic people, the graduation potential model offers an economic rationale why the SOM and Arts and Science schism was strong at DSU.

Premises

Premises or conjectures are the scientific or business assumptions you make when you set out to do your work. They are especially important in theoretical works for setting up your equations. However, you will find on occasion that your premises or conjectures are wrong once you have the data to test them. You should not be afraid to acknowledge that you had to revise your premises, for you want to maintain your integrity for high-quality research. You may want to use implied premises for audiences accustom to your research area, as oppose to overt premises when they have little knowledge of your discussion field.

The key issue to keep in mind is, "Does the reader understand my assumptions?" If you worry that the reader does not appreciate your assumptions, you might opt for overt premises.

The premises section of the Detroit Rubber Group paper reads:

> An assessment of the literature and discussions with hose industry experts suggest a set of premises for coupling textile reinforced high pressure hoses. They are:
>
> 1. Frictional force is the dominant force in fitting retention.
>
> 2. If the ferrule is screwed into the filament bundle, it could cause a significant loss of reinforcement cord tensile strength increasing the potential of hose fitting failures.
>
> 3. Filament transverse tensile modulus is a key contributor to the compressional force necessary for fitting retention.
>
> 4. Hose fitting design is a proprietary art of the fitting manufacturers
>
> 5. Adhesion between both the cover jacket and the inner-liner with the reinforcement for elastomeric compounds is necessary to avoid unnecessary displacement of the liner during swaging.

The focus of the above premises is on an experimental effort. You will note a different slant in ones intended for theoretical calculations. They highlight the importance of premises in deriving equations because you must have a foundation upon which to build your mathematical model.

The following came from the paper entitled, "Knitted Heater Hose Static Equations: Burst Pressure and Economics":

To derive the above equation required adopting three premises. They are:

> 1. Cord bundle cross section area remained constant regardless of cord tension and simulated inner-liner outside diameter.
>
> 2. Cord bundle modification (aspect) ratio is greater than one
>
> 3. Cord gauge is a function of the bundle modification ratio, denier (dtex), and cord density."
>
> The first premise addressed what happens to the cord bundle when the reinforcement cord undergoes tensioning while it is around the inner-liner. Previous work assumed the face area of the cord bundle remains constant. Since the cord length remains unchanged, the constant face area assumption utilizes the rationale of Poisson's ratio where the total bundle volume remains constant after the material deforms.
>
> The second premise merely implies that the bundle will not be round. A round bundle has a modification ratio of 1 and is indicative of high twisted cord.
>
> The third premise spells out the key cord bundle factors believed related to its gauge.

Below are the assumptions used in my Delaware State University study:

> i. All students enrolled in the business calculus classes are capable of handling the course work and the instructor's role is to guide their development.
>
> ii. Fifty percent of the class or more may have educational background deficiencies that necessitate a less-chance student teaching strategy to improve the course pass rate.

iii. Many students may not have learned how effectively to study a mathematics textbook and often may not appreciate the distinction between reading a scientific text and other types of written works (e.g., novels, newspapers, etc.).

iv. Many students may act preemptively and drop the course as early as after the first test because they conclude failure is inevitable.

v. Mathematics professors may teach business calculus with a significant mathematics or hard science slant while rarely demonstrating the mathematics' usage in the business world.

vi. Business students need a capstone experience involving the use of the mathematics that they learned during the semester.

vii. The cooperative learning style of instruction offers a starting point on which to develop a teaching style for background deficient business calculus students.

viii. Lecturers should be aware that the development of background deficient students over the course of the class might follow the Exponential Teaching Model rather than a straight-line curve where the material coverage pages p is a function of t the weeks in the semester or session $p = cA^{\frac{t}{\mu}}$ and c and μ are constants (Miller, 2005, p.162).

ix. Lecturers should teach a maximum of 40% of the class period leaving a significant portion of time for problem solving with the class.

x. Blackboard assignments offer a gauge to help to assess an individual student's learning effort and ensure the student understands the course material under discussion.

xi. Many students may need to meet an acculturation to mainstream performance expectation.

xii. Quasi-ethnographer student assessments (i.e., lecturer studies student's eyes, expressions, and gestures following her or his query of the student's understanding) become a gauge of the student understandings of the course material in the lectures.

xiii. The exact course outline should be flexible so that the particular interests of the class are an integral portion of the course. This may increase the overall passion of the students for the course.

xiv. There is a relationship between time until first test and the student dropout rate in the class.

Objectives

Objectives are precise goals your research advisor wants you to achieve with your research effort. They bring focus to your doctoral thesis or dissertation because they allow your advisor to quickly conclude whether you have achieved something of doctoral caliber. Your research advisor and doctoral committee members can also use your objectives as a gauge to determine whether your research solved the problem or problems that you agreed to study.

Once you start your research effort, you may need to renegotiate the objectives, since your findings might suggest that the initial set of goals were unrealistic. You also need very clear objectives because they enhance your ability to write the doctoral thesis or dissertation quickly, since your writing effort can focus on answering the questions posed by these objectives. If your writing is focused around your objectives, you will find that your data is prioritized and allows you to avoid the confusion associated with information overload.

Discussion

The Discussion section gives you an opportunity to present your findings in detail. This is where you discuss your test design, make your calculations, and present your data. You are providing information that shows how you met the goal or goals that you raised in the Introduction section.

There are many ways to layout the discussion section, but the following sub-areas may be present in many reports:

a) Opening Comments
b) Background
c) Test Outline
d) Data
e) Results

Opening Comments

Opening comments are your last-ditch effort to capture your reader's mind to spend the time necessary to read through the material you are about to present. These statements succinctly restate ideas that you presented elsewhere in the report but are worthy of repetition. An example of an opening comment is:

> Du Pont's initial study of automotive coolant and heater hoses focused on knitted heater hoses. In this effort Du Pont examined hose construction parameters in both static and dynamic tests on hoses reinforced with Nomex®, Kevlar®, and Technora® Aramid.
>
> Although Du Pont ran both static and dynamic tests on knitted heater hoses, this paper will only utilize the results of the static phase of this program. . . .

We look at a second technical opening comment to see another example of how this sub area encourages your readers to read your work by offering them some comforting language. The use of scientific terms known by many disciplines in this opening section gives your readership an appreciation of your ideas in familiar language. The technical paper entitled, "Aramid Transverse Filament Properties and Hose Fitting Retention" provides an example of how you can use this familiar language to entice your audience to wade through a lengthy section of your trade paper or internal technical report:

> Steel wire hose reinforcement is often made up of monofilament cord bundles lying adjacent to one another.

> These large bundles may sustain ferrule penetration without a great deal of loss in their tensile strength.
>
> Textile cord bundles are usually made up of many small filaments that are its fundamental building units. The strength of the textile cord bundle is a function of what percent of these filaments break at one time.
>
> Significant damage to fiber filaments during installation could lower the strength of the textile cord bundle thereby reducing its fitting retention capability. This suggests that filament damage studies must be done prior to accepting screwed-on fittings for multifilament textile reinforced hoses.
>
> Swaged fittings are more appropriate for textile reinforcements because they rely solely on compressional forces for fitting retention. Figure 3 offers a pictorial representation of these forces where the large arrows are swage nodes. Frictional forces between the hose and the fitting components are the principal retaining mechanism for fitting retention.
>
> This paper starts examining the contributions to the frictional force retaining the fitting. It assumes that the static friction equation is applicable in the analysis of the fitting retention.
>
> The filament is the fundamental building unit of the multifilament textile bundle, so an examination of the filament's transverse deformation with an applied stress offers some insight on fitting retention. Understanding the characteristics of this deformation helps in an appreciation of the normal force component in the friction equation governing the hose fitting retention during hose pressurization (Miller, 1993).

This paper uses terms that touch the textile, steel wire and hose industries. The intent is to start supplying the reinforcement knowledge to the hose manufacturers that allows them to replace heavy steel wire reinforcement with light-weight, high-strength textiles. Since the paper's target audience is hose manufacturers and hose users, you have merely supplied the new knowledge in language that they can understand.

A portion of the Discussion section from my doctoral thesis offers a guide on this section viewed from a social science prospectus.

> "In developing insights to solve the Delaware State University high failure rate problems in finite mathematics and business calculus, an appreciation of the plight of the native-born African Americans in the mainstream American educational arena may underpin a mindset for teaching African American students. The historical legacy of the State of Delaware on educating its African American citizens need highlighting to capture the heritage in which Delaware State University offers educational opportunities to today's black students.
>
> This section presents features of the approach recommended on the basis of this project as responses to the continuing situation for these students, which must be understood as part of Delaware's historical legacy."

Students' African American Heritage and the Wulff Misalignment Model

The course taking history in Tables 1 and 2 (pages 16 and 18 respectively) suggests that many Delaware State University business students may be enrolling in mathematics for which their backgrounds are inadequate to be successful. The students' use of this deficit background practice means that DSU teachers employing solely yesteryear's direct instruction style may find a very difficult time motivating today's students to be successful in their courses. A key problem is that some teachers may be teaching based on where the students' academic backgrounds should be versus where they actually are. This suggests what Donald H. Wulff would term a misalignment between the teachers, the students, and the content (Wulff, 2005).

In examining the components of the Wulff misalignment model using the Delaware State University high failure rate problems for finite mathematics and business calculus as an underpinning, we get some insights that may offer future direction in resolving this crisis. Delaware State University's President Allen Sessoms defined the student market for the university in speaking to its African American heritage. 'Delaware State University embraces its heritage as a historically black university. There are no plans to depart from that mission. In fact, this year's incoming freshmen class currently reflects 74 percent African-American, a reflection of the university's recruiting efforts' (Sessoms, 2005).

Greene and Winters, writing for The Manhattan Institute, share that 23 percent of African American students graduating from high school are college ready. The evolution away from yesteryear's racially segregated colleges and universities that guaranteed historically black colleges a monopoly in educating African American students now finds Delaware State University in a competitive environment for today's academically strong African American students. Traditionally White Colleges are recruiting qualified African Americans to diversify their student body. This means that Delaware State University may need efforts to handle average African American high school graduates. . .

Background

The background offers you an opportunity to tell of preliminary efforts you undertook that helped to define your premises or the experiments you elected to run. It is especially important to elaborate on joint efforts with co-workers or offer a chronology of efforts that led you to do this work. The background section is very important when you are making presentations to specific groups at your doctoral chairperson's request who are interested in your research effort and when you wish to remind everyone of work done in the past. This saves attendees at your doctoral seminars and readers of your doctoral thesis or dissertation from straining their memories, and avoids numerous questions where your audience has little knowledge of your past efforts. It also avoids the distractions associated with one or two persons bringing their detailed notes from previous seminars, thus making others feel insecure because they do not have comparable information.

On occasion, a background section enhances the clarity of the ideas you present in your thesis. An example of this is seen in the following comments on the idea of textile filament transverse properties as significant in hose fitting retention:

> An appreciation of hose coupling mechanisms and the acceptance that single filaments are the fundamental components of the multifilament hose reinforcement bundle lead to the hypothesis that the mechanical properties of the reinforcing filaments normal to their longitudinal axis influence coupling retention performance. Experiments were run to estimate these transverse mechanical properties of Aramid reinforcing fibers and to develop a better understanding of the structural variables that influence them.

In a social science setting a background could entail a history of events you believe contribute to the problems you are attempting to resolve. Consider a brief history of African Americans experience in the economic mainstream from my doctoral thesis that highlights key events in black history with a slant to Delaware History.

> *Some key racial epochs in US History offer some feel for the native-born blacks' distrust:*
>
> 1. The 1896 U.S. Supreme Court ruling in the Plessy vs. Ferguson case legalized racial segregation, dashing the hopes of Black America ever gaining entrance into the economic mainstream on an equal footing.
>
> 2. The State of Delaware exploited this separate but equal epoch. "In the late 19th century, the state Legislature with great reluctance agreed that the state would support education for black people. But their reluctance was so overwhelming that the law that created state schools for blacks said they'd be paid for from a special fund that would be collected from black people, from taxes on land owned by blacks, and only black people would be taxed to support the black schools." (Tristam,1999).
>
> 3. Time Magazine reported on January 31, 1927, that Pierre DuPont had spent five million dollars to build all of the Negro schools in Delaware. (Finis, 1927).

4. Drew Ostroski sums up Pierre DuPont's impact on higher education for blacks in the State of Delaware. He reports in 1931 that Pierre DuPont bought beds, linens, furniture for then Delaware State College and installed a sewage system. 'You could even say he saved the college because it was just barely alive' (Ostroski).

5. The racially integrated public schools purportedly arrived with the unanimous May 17, 1954, U.S. Supreme Court ruling banning racial segregation in public schools. Julie Kailin offers the unintended consequences of the Brown vs. Board of Education ruling. 'For one of the unintended effects of the 1954 Brown v. Board of Education decision was that, due to entrenched White racism, many African American teachers were fired in the South in the newly desegregated schools and were unwelcome in the North. . . The time-worn myth that it really doesn't matter what you do because 'these people do not value education' is deeply ingrained in the thinking of many White Americans regarding African Americans. Most White Americans are ignorant of the reality of education as a tool of the struggle historically in the African American community' (Kailin, 1999).

6. Gary Orfield, Mark Bachmeier, David R. James, and Tamela Eitle offer a regressive picture of public school integration in the late 1990s. They highlight the role of the current U.S. Supreme Court in exacerbating racial and ethnic segregation in America.

7. "The appointment of Justice Clarence Thomas in 1991 consolidated a majority favoring cutting back civil rights remedies requiring court-ordered changes in racial patterns. . ."

It may be that the 'separate but equal' euphemism from the 1896 US Supreme Court ruling in the Plessy vs. Ferguson case morphed into continued poor quality education for African Americans in the public school systems. The percentage of Black students graduating from high school college-ready is a barometer of the long-term socioeconomic upward mobility potential of Black

Americans. Jay P. Greene and Marcus Winters, writing for The Manhattan Institute, reported:

1. About 40% of white students, 23% of African-American students, and 20% of Hispanic students who started public high school graduated college-ready in 2002.

2. There is very little difference between the number of students who graduate from high school college-ready and the number of students who enroll in college for the first time. . . (Greene & Winters, 2005).

This brief history of the adverse impact on black Americans seeking public education suggests that many native-born African American students may harbor distrust of the public educational system. Delaware has an especially insalubrious history in denying blacks access to quality education, so Delaware State University's historical black heritage continues to be a symbol of hope of a better tomorrow in the State of Delaware. Yet yesterday's racist actions perpetrated by mainstream political leaders against African American upward mobility may enchant some African American students into accepting the stereotypic image of their incapability to handle academic endeavors. Today's teachers of African American students may need strategies for kindling the pursuit of academic excellence in these students. In appreciating this injurious history of native-born African Americans' educational difficulty, it is important not to give today's African American students an opportunity to exploit this racial suffering as a scapegoat to justify their nonperformance in mathematics courses. .

Test Outline

You should make a test outline of how you intend to present your data, remembering that it should tell a story. If your readers recognize that you are about to present a clear narrative, they will feel comfortable following your logic to see how it unfolds. Their comfort with your story enhances the chances they will read your paper, report, or thesis. There are two key aspects in this section:

a) Present your experimental test design, and

b) Tell about any unique equipment you used to make measurements.

I will continue to use an example from my doctoral thesis.

Appendix C offers a discussion of class projects that gives the evolution of a testing style. "Since it was apparent that direct instruction was not going to produce my desired learning result, I started to look for ways to lower the student to teacher ratio and increase the material coverage of the business calculus course. I needed some practical schemes that the students would embrace without my appearing to be condescending in their view. I decided to give the business calculus students a semester project similar to the finite mathematics students.

The ground rules for the business calculus project was that the students must use some portion of the mathematics they learned during the semester to solve a real world problem. Students were not limited to any portion of the mathematics. My goal was to see what the students had passion about; so I gave them the freedom to use their creativity.

During the presentations, I challenged people to defend their work. People could only take their charts or write out their problem on the blackboard. Some people made up charts but most people developed their problem on the blackboard while others were speaking. This technique caused some distraction but in the interest of time, it was our best approach.

People were required to give their presentation in a business manner. Many people came dressed for the occasion as if they were giving a formal presentation.

A holistic look at the results of the oral presentation suggested that students presented material at the level of what I would expect of finite mathematics students. Only one student gave a calculus level presentation. My dismay was that the students were not seeing business calculus as another tool in their repertoire or they felt very uncomfortable with the calculus principles covered during the semester. I concluded that the finite mathematics presentation model was not successful with business calculus students. I wanted to continue with the presentation concept, but it needed redesigning to force the students to show their appreciation of business calculus. . .

Data

There are many different ways to present your data. You must find the system with which you are comfortable. However, you want to make certain that you are presenting sufficient data to support your case.

Table 5.1

CORD BUNDLE FACE AREA COMPARISON MEASUREMENT

DENIER	BAR SIZE (MM)	CORD TENSION (GRAMS)	AREA (MM SQ.)	AREA INCREASE (%)
1000	0	454	0.1337	0
1000	12.7	454	0.1736	30
1000	9.7	454	0.1888	41
1000	12.7	1816	0.1816	36
1000	9.7	1816	0.2072	55
2250	0	454	0.333	0
2250	12.7	454	0.4284	29
2250	9.7	454	0.4634	39

* SMALLEST BAR SIZE HAS GREATEST FACE AREA
* HIGHER TENSION INCREASES FACE AREA
* AVERAGE FACE AREA INCREASE ACROSS ALL BARS IS ~38%
* COMPARABLE AREA INCREASE AT CONSTANT TENSION

You want to keep in mind that data and chart portability are underpinning goals in your coursework papers. You want to include an analysis of the data on charts, graphs, and tables. Tables like Table 5.1 offer maximum portability between research papers, articles, presentations, and theses because it can be converted into a standalone chart to report your findings.

Including insignificant data to impress people with the amount of work you did makes your course work papers, thesis and trade publications very uninteresting and even confusing to your audience. You want to avoid this practice, for you can make your potential readership shun reading your entire thesis, paper or report. Audiences instinctively may see your works through the adage that success is inversely proportional to the thickness of the report.

Results

The results section provides the findings from your experiments or theoretical calculations and discusses them in detail, along with how you achieved your goal/objective. You make the case for your position or insight, and use your data to support this belief. You may also need to call upon the works of others in this section to support your belief.

An example of a short results section that highlighted the importance of transverse filament properties in high pressure hose fitting retention follows:

> At 25 degrees C, the transverse tensile modulus of the KEVLAR® fibers shows a generally increasing trend from 1.6 Gpa (232 kpsi) for the lowest crystallinity KEVLAR© 129, to 2.4 GPa (348 kpsi) for the highest crystallinity KEVLAR© 149. The modulus of PPD/PQP-T commercial copolymer at 1.2 GPa (174 kpsi) is significantly lower than any of the KEVLAR® samples.
>
> At 100 degrees C, the difference between the KEVLAR® and the PPD/POP-T copolymer is even more dramatic. Whereas the transverse modulus of the KEVLAR® did not change significantly, the modulus of the PPD/POP-T copolymer decreased ~25% from 1.2 GPa (174 kpsi) to 0.9 GPa (131 kpsi). This difference in response to elevated temperature between the KEVLAR® and the copolymer fiber is not surprising in view of the very low crystallinity of the PPD/POP-T copolymer compared to the KEVLAR®. The above results also offer an explanation to findings reported by DuPont Toray Kevlar to an experiment with high pressure hoses reinforced with either KEVLAR® 129 or PPD/POP-T commercial copolymer. The design burst pressure of these hoses is 1200 kg/cm^2 (roughly 17.4 kpsi). Figure 10 shows that the

> PPD/POP-T copolymer hose failed prematurely and the KEVLAR® 129 achieved the hose burst pressure goal. A blown off fitting was the premature failure mode. A similar experience has also been reported in the United States of America.
>
> These preliminary experiments suggest the potential importance of the transverse modulus of the yarn filaments. However, more testing is needed to insure that fitting installation problems or improper fitting selection are ruled out as a cause of these premature fitting failure findings. .

In a social science thesis one may find results reported comparable to:

> The key goal of the oral presentation phase was to force the students to make presentations on the advance material in the business calculus course. If my goal was to solely look at the effects of cooperative learning, I may have created teams made up of people randomly selected. However, [Tables] suggest that I could not risk having teams made up with people with large academic preparation deficits. I worried about the potential of students feeling overwhelmed should I have teams made up of all background deficit people. I decided to use the written tests to identify academically strong students who I would spread amongst the various teams. Students initially picked their initial team members and then I balanced the teams with the strong students.
>
> Since no one knew who would be the presenter for their team, the pressure mounted for everyone to be prepared. I first covered all of the sections on differential calculus of one variable in the textbook. I then devised two problems for each team that may be too difficult for anyone student to do quickly. The students were given a week to do the problems and turn in these problems for me to grade. I graded the problems harshly but I did not return the papers to the students until after the oral presentations. The presenters understood if they got the problem right and their team got it wrong they would get the higher credit.

Conclusion

There is always some confusion over the difference between the conclusion section and the summary section of technical reports or trade articles. In the conclusion section you want to state specifically what you concluded from your research effort. It should consist of a few succinct statements that leave no doubt as to what you believe your data means or does not mean.

Let us continue our Kevlar® filament transverse modulus discussion by looking at an example of a conclusion section:

> The transverse modulus of a fiber is a measure of its ability to resist transverse deformation and also the amount of stress generated under a given deformation. In view of our current understanding of the mechanism of hose fitting retention, transverse modulus appears to be a fundamental fiber property that is relevant to textile reinforced high pressure hose performance. The data presented above suggest that KEVLAR® Aramid fiber has superior transverse properties which will provide better hose fitting retention performance.
>
> These experiments represent initial efforts to relate fiber properties to hose fitting performance retention. In order to develop a more complete understanding, experiments to determine time dependent transverse properties (stress relaxation or creep) at hose operating temperatures are needed.

Summary

The summary section is a holistic look at what you reported. In this section you touch on the salient points of your research to ensure that your readers have an overall picture of what was done. This section is very important in that many potential readers may read only the abstract and summary or conclusion prior to deciding to invest time and effort in reading your entire paper.

There are two types of summaries that you should consider in presenting your findings or recommendations in reports and theses. They are the simple summary and the executive summary.

When you are writing long documents or you have a great deal of data, you may want to offer your audience an executive summary in the front of the report where you give a brief overview of the data or findings. Doctoral candidates may also find that writing a succinct executive summary helps to give you a clear picture of the value of your findings and recommendations to your intended audience and may highlight holes in your research effort.

An executive summary might read:

> This inquiry offers teaching techniques for handling background deficient mathematics students (those students with poor understanding of fundamental mathematics, such as, algebra) in both finite mathematics and business calculus. The supporting research confirms that direct instruction, when coupled with blackboard assignments, can be a satisfactory instructional technique for teaching finite mathematics to background deficient students if the instructor takes advantage of the significant overlap between finite mathematics and algebra to bridge academic deficiencies during the semester. A cooperative learning style is presented as the preferred choice for business calculus students because the complexity of calculus relies heavily on a solid mathematics foundation and the impersonality of direct teaching appears to exacerbate the already low morale of students facing the class without sufficient preparation. In addition, requiring the students to demonstrate excellence in the subject areas is surmised to increase the course pass rates in finite mathematics and business calculus. Test cases include classes where finite mathematics students were encouraged to seek an industrial level of excellence by making presentations in a quasi-capstone experience and business calculus students demonstrated their pursuit of excellence through tough team take-home examinations that included individual accountability.
>
> Quantitative measures in this inquiry include percent pass rate and course dropout rate. In particular with business calculus, the goal was to the help business students achieve an eighty percent pass rate in the class with sixty percent of the students earning a "C" or better grade. Student dropout rate in both business calculus and finite mathematics classes studied here averaged roughly

ten percent when the Modified Bragg grading system (dropping the first or second in-class examination in figuring out the final course grade), the Exponential Teaching model, and the aforementioned teaching styles were employed.

Research summary might read:

I set out initially to help to reduce an estimated fifty percent failure rate in business calculus by business majors at Delaware State University. I suspected that background deficiencies in the subject area were the cause so my hope was to develop ways to help background deficient students reach a pass rate of at least eighty percent. However, I came to conclude that being my primary objective merely got students passing the business calculus course but it did not encourage their pursuit of excellence. Based on my twenty years of industrial experience working in technical marketing, manufacturing, and end-use research at the E. I. DuPont De Nemours & Company Inc. where I made presentations in many nations, I knew what was necessary to be successful in business and felt my teaching objective should be to encourage business calculus students to pursue excellence. If students learn to pursue excellence as their norm, then higher pass rates would fall out as a necessary consequence.

Therefore, I felt that I could not focus my attention solely on a discussion of business calculus. I needed to look at the students' performance in finite mathematics, a precursor to business calculus. Since finite mathematics was usually a freshman level course, I assumed the students would be more impressionable than business calculus students. I could affect a reduction in failure rates in business calculus by starting with finite mathematics where I could shape the students' modus operandi. Although I speak about findings in finite mathematics courses, I delimitate my discussion to finite mathematics material that may be important for learning business calculus.

The pedagogical mind-set that underpins my discussion is the need to teach both finite mathematics and business calculus as practical business courses that call for a great deal of mathematics. I hypothesized that a business mind-set would make my lectures more palatable to business students. I attempted to make the material appear as something that business students can use immediately and focused on money issues that may affect a student's personal money or her or his performance on a future job. Esoteric problems, that may be great brainteasers for mathematics majors, were persona non grata in my courses. Mathematical derivations were held to a minimum—offered only where I felt it necessary information for students to understand a business principle under discussion.

In assessing students' blackboard performance, their first examination (algebra review) scores, and their prior course tenures in prerequisite courses for both finite mathematics and business calculus or tenures in the same courses, I was able to gain an assessment of the students' mathematical maturity and guesstimate their desire to embrace academic perseverance. These data suggested that poor academic preparation may be significantly impacting student four year graduation rates because some students repeated several courses. In situations where the students' backgrounds were up to academic standard, they usually performed well in business calculus.

Since one might expect business students to be pragmatic people, I concluded that the primary goal of my research was to help increase the graduation rate potential of school of management students. The focus on graduation rate allowed the increased student pass rate to become a fall out of students' acceptance of academic excellence as their norm.

Kindling Academic Perseverance

Concerned that some students might give up too easily, I devised a scheme to make the decision to drop the course very difficult for students in both finite mathematics and business calculus. For example, I pushed the first written in-class test close to the middle of the semester. The hope was that the students may have felt they had invested too much time into the course to drop at that point.

The students understood that 25 percent of the semester grade came from blackboard assignments. Every student had to be prepared to go to the blackboard on every class meeting to work out problems. Students were only allowed to take their textbook. They were asked to write out the instructions and the problem before attempting to solve it. I enforced this so that it was clear what the problem asked (some students had a tendency to solve what they guess was asked versus what was really asked). I asked students to erase and rewrite things incorrectly written on the blackboard—the goal was to teach the students that I expected a high standard of excellence in all assignments.

Students who did not understand their homework assignments or who had difficulty working the problem in the day's lesson had to remain at the blackboard until they understood the material. Initially, the blackboard caused consternation with some students for it highlighted the severity of their background deficiencies. I worked under the belief that learning is cumulative, so the blackboard experience would eventually turn positive as the semester advanced. As the semester advanced, I found many people wanting to go to the blackboard and asking for additional problems. I regularly reminded the students that my job was to teach the mathematics and not merely to fail people out.

I used the Modified Bragg Grading system in both finite mathematics and business calculus. I dropped the lower of the first two test scores in determining the final grade. I only allowed one of the first two tests to be dropped to encourage students to continue to work up to their potential throughout the semester

Many students who failed at midterm were able to improve their grade by the final grade since the Modified Bragg Grading system offered them hope of still getting a good grade. The goal was to keep hope alive for the students in the midst of a bleak midterm assessment. . .

I employed the exponential teaching model . . . in teaching both finite mathematics and business calculus. This model allowed an opportunity to fill-in background deficiencies in the early portion of the course and pick up the pace for the remainder of the semester. The goal was not to academically overwhelm the class in the early portion of the semester; thereby, the students would have to toil with a decision to drop the course. The student drop out rate ran under ten percent for both finite mathematics and business calculus.

Works Cited

There is some concern over the issue of using footnotes and a bibliography or using endnotes alone. Since the issue that we are addressing here is the reader's ability to find the source materials we used in our thesis, dissertation, trade paper or internal technical report, we opt for using only endnotes in the interest of rapid writing. Footnotes clutter up your pages with redundant information. There really is not an immediate need for this information during the course of the reader's assessment of your report.

A good word processing program generates the endnotes for you as you are including your reference sources into your paper. This feature is invaluable, for it will number your references automatically and even renumber them if you have to include a new reference source in a later revision of your report, thesis, or dissertation.

You can adopt standard formats for your endnotes found in many English textbooks. The important issue is to be consistent once you have selected a system to follow. Whichever system you select, it should include the name of the author or authors, the name of the publication, the name of the article or book, date of the article or edition of the book, volume number, and page numbers. If you are using Internet references, you also need to include the URL and the date you retrieved the references.

Graduate students should follow their university's guidelines as to what reference system to use in writing your thesis or dissertation. You may also want to check with major publications to get their guidelines on formatting documents for publication consideration.

An example of an **APA** style Works Cited is:

2005 Achieving the Dream Community Colleges Count. (2005). What is Achieving the Dream? [WWW document] URL http://www.achievingthedream.org/default.tp?tab=college

College Board, SAT. (2006). *2006 College-Bound Seniors State Profile Report DELAWARE* (002_8_STP_01 200). New York [WWW document] URL http://www.collegeboard.com/prod_downloads/about/news_info/cbsenior/yr2006/delaware-2006.pdf

Finis (1927, January 31). *Feudal Delaware*. [WWW document] URLhttp://www.time.com/time/printout/0,8816,729904,00.html

Greene, J. and Winters, M. (2005). *Public High School Graduation and College-Readiness Rates: 1991–2002.* [WWW document] URL http://www.manhattan-institute.org/pdf/ewp_08.pdf

Kailin, J. (1999). How White Teachers Perceive the Problem of Racism in Their Schools: A Case Study in "Liberal" Lakeview. [WWW document] URL http://www.tcrecord.org/Content.asp?ContentID=10340

Miller, S. (2005). Teaching College Algebra Reversing the Effects of Social Promotion. Lanham, Maryland: Rowman & Littlefield Education.

On the other hand, an **ISO 690 Numerical Reference** Bibliography might look like this:

1. African Americans - Lynchings, The Lynching of Sam Hose. *AfricanAmericans.com.* [Online] 2007. [Cited: June 30, 2008.] http://www.africanamericans.com/SamHose.htm.

2. Hip-Hop Style. *NewsHour's Hip-Hop report.* [Online] [Cited: July 7, 2007.] http://www.pbs.org/newshour/infocus/fashion/hiphop.html.

3. Human Rights Report World Report 2003: United States . *HRW.org.* [Online] 2006. [Cited: July 5, 2007.] http://www.hrw.org/wr2k3/us.html .

4. **Bernhardt, Victoria, L.** *Data Analysis for Continous School Improvement.* Larchmont : Eye on Education, Inc. , 2004.

Closing

Clarity of our vision and defining the writing elements are key ingredients in our ability to write our doctoral theses and business reports in timely manners. In addition to defining the writing elements, both hard and social science examples are offered as guides to aid in our writing effort. Our writing template is now functional. Thus, we are now ready for some completion adages that will help to keep our attention on the writing task we are about to undertake.

Chapter VI

Doctoral Thesis Completion Adages

As we develop our writing skills, we learn to call upon some rules of thumb to aid in discovering our own personal writing style. You will no doubt get many words of wisdom on writing from many people. I garnered my share of this advice over the years, and generated a few of my own that were the fallout of my own writing efforts. Some adages and ideas that I found to be useful in getting in the right frame of mind to produce professional publications and charts for senior management reviews and doctoral committee members are given in this chapter.

Use only those adages that make sense to you as writing aids, though it may be helpful if you at least try others on for size before you discard them. You want to avoid prematurely ignoring ideas that may help improve your writing productivity. Perhaps you can develop a series of these adages to meet your own personal writing needs as your writing proficiency improves.

Five minutes' worth of thinking is worth five hours of writing.

All writing first takes place in your mind. You begin by building a mental image of how you want things to be when your work is published and presented. This mental image becomes the blueprint from which you develop your project and the framework which allows you to easily prioritize the data you collect during your research effort. Thus, your brain is clearly the most important central processing unit for any data you generate or locate.

The short time it takes to think through your goal will benefit you tenfold in your writing efforts, since you know what information is important to keep and what to discard. Your writing effort has focus. It is tantamount to addressing a problem like a laser beam aimed at a far distance object.

> The brain is like a muscle; it hurts when you first start to use it but it gets keener with regular exercise, making the mind perform at extraordinary levels.

The brain offers directions to our efforts, and everything else is merely a tool to clarify the vision in our minds. It is common knowledge that the development and use of our own brain is paramount to our upward mobility in the economic mainstream. Yet it is often forgotten that developing the brain can be a painful process and may be ignored by many people when it comes to producing your doctoral thesis, dissertation or report.

The use of your brain is imperative in assessing any data you generate. Unless you have an idea of what you are seeking, all of the data in the world will be useless to you. You must understand thoroughly what you want to communicate, or you will find yourself merely wasting time scribbling on a note pad with little to show for your effort. Some might say you are suffering from writer's block.

If your goal is to get a doctoral degree in a timely manner, you cannot afford to be like an ill-prepared minister I once encountered on a community-based television show. When this minister was asked if he prepared his sermons before he went on air, he replied, "I just let the spirit hit me when I'm on the air." His response left me perplexed, for I had been taught that ministers were to teach all nations, and that meant one had to prepare his or her sermons ahead of time. Clearly you must be willing to put quality work into forming your ideas and not sit haplessly awaiting a celestial revelation.

Discover all of those activities that are catalysts to your thinking process; tasks as simple as washing dishes, running, listening to music, playing tennis, or fishing, to mention a few. Some people even do their best thinking during the minister's homily on Sunday mornings. You should be alert to activities that get your mind active.

The idea is to find ways of feeling good about writing the work you have in front of you. Don't look for excuses that suggest that you are incapable of completing your thesis, dissertation or report where you have invested so much time and energy. I believe that procrastination is like an addictive drug; once you get hooked on it, failure becomes a self fulfilling prophecy.

There should be only one overarching theme per thesis.

If you are sitting and listening to a speaker who offers you three central themes to follow, what do you get from the presentation? I am reminded of going to listen to a presentation by a certain professor. This professor's entire presentation consisted of quotes from famous people. I found myself wondering just what this speaker personally had to offer and what this particular talk was supposed to convey. I couldn't accept this display of confusion, so I asked the professor, "What do you think on this subject?" I am still waiting for an answer.

This professor had a very high fog factor in her work, or was afraid to take any definitive positions. This is probably a worst-case scenario and most people are not nearly this bad, but it does illustrate how one can spread more confusion than enlightenment by not having one overarching theme.

You should work hard to leave a clear message in the minds of your audience. If you have more than one message, the audience will have difficulty sorting through your data. Furthermore, your central theme gets lost in these secondary agendas.

A central theme also culls your data. It forces you to ask, "Does this information support the message I am attempting to convey to my audience?"

When in doubt, leave it out!

When writing a report to senior management or a thesis for doctoral committee review, if you find yourself debating whether or not to put in a piece of questionable data, don't! Your doctoral thesis or reports to senior management should not contain any information that you cannot explain. If the data happens to be wrong, your credibility will be lost, and it takes a very long time to regain it. Furthermore, people feel warmly toward you if they think each paragraph in your thesis, article or report is rich with information.

Know the medium through which you intend to publish a given article or report and the audience's background.

If you are writing a doctoral thesis, you want to know something about any idiosyncrasies on your doctoral committee to avoid committing a faux pas that may encumber your degree pursuit.

Some technical journals make it very clear that they do not want sales articles. These journals are in the business of sharing scientific findings, and they may abhor sales types trying to exploit their journals as sales mediums. The Journal of the Society of Automotive Engineers (SAE) might be considered an example of a sterile scientific journal used by global corporations to report findings on their internal research efforts. The SAE has gone so far as to require that an author use only generic names for products to avoid sales pitches for specific brand names.

Conversely, writing a solely technical article for a media aimed at marketing executives may only find your work dropped into the editor's trash can, and a polite refusal letter. When you are writing your doctoral thesis you need to be mindful of the slant of the doctoral committee. If you are getting a doctoral degree in leadership, then your thesis needs to show something in the leadership realm that you have accomplished. If you are getting the doctorate in solid state physics, then your committee will expect to see some discovery that you made. A presentation before your doctoral committee is no place for you to be promoting your personal agenda if it does not align with the agreement that you made with your advisor in developing your doctoral thesis or dissertation topic. Unnecessary friction between you and your doctoral committee chairperson or other committee members may encumber your effort to gain signatures from your committee members that attest that you have passed your oral thesis defense. Your goal is to not kowtow but be perceived as a peer with the committee members wanting to welcome you into their society of experts.

Back up your work every day.

I find it helpful to save my work on two different storage units when working at home; the hard drive of my computer and a USB Flash Drive. I keep the flash drive with me. I also find it good practice to email copies of my upgrades to a family member who is on a completely different computer system in case my systems are destroyed by some ill-fated act. Saving your work in multiple places reduces your daily worries of seeing perhaps a year's work destroyed.

Do not write confidential white papers on non-secure personal computers or workstations.

Today, industrial espionage is a way of life. Trade secrets, such as recipes for new products or strategic directions planned by a corporation, can be worth hundreds of millions of dollars. Its human cost can mean the loss of thousands of jobs as global competitors nibble at your corporation's market share.

Undoubtedly, computers are godsends to the rapid development of your publication, but they are also prime sources for others to steal your confidential ideas and findings. Many people instinctively save their work on a hard disk drive or a memory stick, for it is very quick and easy to do. Some people also remember to put a password on this information to feel reasonably sure that no one can get to their secret. A false sense of security may lead them to tell others that they are working on very confidential projects.

You should keep in mind that good computer hackers garner great pleasure in cracking your password. The best security against this is to say nothing to anyone other than your immediate team members about even the existence of your project. There is an old adage appropriate to today's competitive global corporate society: "Loose lips sink ships."

Thus, you should have in place provisions to discard hard copies of your report and to destroy CDs or DVDs used during your writing. Saving information on the hard disk drive should be kept to a minimum, for deleting does not remove it from this disk, especially with modern operating systems that emphasize easy recovery as a feature. The stationary hard disk offers a beachhead for a computer hacker to initiate their search to locate your information.

We all marvel at how powerful laptop computers have become. Today, high-end laptops rival yesterday's workstations in their capabilities, and that makes them of great interest to industrial spies. If you are writing on a laptop and store your work on its hard disk drive, you offer industrial spies an opportunity to steal your secrets by simply stealing your computer or finding ways to gain access to it while you are, perhaps out of your hotel room entertaining customers. A good hacker could simply duplicate the information on your hard drive and work on cracking it later.

As laptops move toward having tetrabyte hard drives in the near future, you want to ask yourself, "Could my corporation afford to lose a tetrabyte of confidential data?" If you are using your laptop to write confidential reports at home, you may wish to restrict the saving of your reports to CD-Rs, removable hard drives, or transferring to external storage units that remain at your home.

Imagine the reaction reflected in your workmates' faces if they found out that your carelessness caused corporate secrets to be stolen by foreign competitors, which could, in turn, cost them their jobs. There is no doubt that you would have a difficult time with people knowing you caused the latest round of downsizing at your corporation.

If you are doing doctoral research in an area where there are other groups competing to show positive results on the same issues be mindful to ensure critical data is released on the schedule you think is best. Your results could save other teams countless hours of research, yet not benefit you without the proper system in place to guarantee your recognition. Once it is clear that you will receive recognition for your discoveries, use them to write up your doctoral thesis or dissertation and also share these discoveries with the general public.

User-friendly articles and reports get read more often than stereotypical technocratic jargon.

Although the doctoral thesis or dissertation must be written at the academic level that is appropriate for the degree being sought, you should write with the idea of making your work accessible to people who are not members of your peer group. User-friendliness is the most difficult aspect of thesis and technical writing, for it requires you to have an understanding of the subject matter and a willingness to share this information with a mass audience.

If you have a case where someone truly understands his or her subject matter, yet feels insecure in his or her job position, he or she may become an expert at gobbledygook. I once visited a customer accompanied by a highly technical corporate associate to assist in solving a development problem, yet after he left, I spent the next three months translating his technical presentation to the customer. The words of the customer still ring in my mind: "What did he say?"

This same associate refused to offer any assistance that allowed one to truly understand his research work. His reluctance to share data and understanding brought into question his true worth to the organization, and made me wonder if he maintained a high fog factor to purposefully keep the company from making a cost/benefit analysis of his projects.

On the other hand, you hear people comment, "I was totally lost while listening to that presentation, and there was no doubt in my mind that the speaker had no idea what he was doing." It is embarrassing to see a person writing about something of which he or she has no knowledge, and having someone else point out the writer's ignorance. People in the scientific community are not bashful when they think you are wrong. I learned that at an international conference on solid state physics when a world renowned physicist corrected a presenter's paper on the stage.

A similar situation occurs during internal presentations and reports when a scientist or engineer publishes questionable data that a senior member in their organization knows is wrong, or when they have incomplete data that does not answer the question that their corporate management or doctoral committee chairperson posed for their research. In each case, the researcher is essentially lying, for they are knowingly presenting false information to their management or doctoral committee.

Thus, if you decide that a key goal of your work is for your extended audience to be able to use your data immediately, user-friendliness becomes a labor of love. If you are making a theoretical derivation, add the couple of extra lines that will save the reader valuable time trying to work through your calculations.

User-friendliness implies that you stay focused on the issue at hand. This will avoid confusing the reader while you engage in a digression that may add very little value to your thesis, article or report. Remember that people instinctively gauge the success of your work by its brevity, so you do not want them to ignore your thesis, paper or report because you're padding it with confusing and irrelevant information.

User-friendliness can also apply to the language used to write your thesis, report or article. While working for the DuPont Company, I experimented with using my journalistic experience to make technical reports readable as well as to produce them very quickly. When my reviewer read my earlier reports, he complained about my writing style. My goal was to make a shift in the readability of technical reports, so I set about utilizing the system being developed in this book. Over time our technical director commented to me how much he enjoyed reading my technical reports.

My focus was to take complicated ideas and break them down as I would if I were writing a newspaper column. The key goal was to have the audience understand my research and to report only the significant data needed to make my case.

It became apparent that writing in the active voice turned dull reading into interesting material. This style of writing makes the reader feel the action is occurring today and not something that was done a hundred years ago.

I also found that paragraphs should average three to four sentences in length with a maximum of six sentences, with the font at 12 points for ease of reading. Each sentence should average no more than five lines on 8 1/2 by 11 inch (22 x 28 cm) paper with a one inch (2.5 cm) margin at the top, bottom, left, and right.

A picture is worth a thousand words.

Graphics negate the need to use several pages of text to visualize difficult concepts. They also transcend language barriers within your university community and corporation or at international conferences.

Graphics can be tables, charts, and/or pictures within the same document. More than one central idea per chart can lead your audience to erroneous conclusions. Whenever possible, put a conclusion below the graphic. This will ensure that the reader will come to your desired conclusion and not merely interpret your findings using only their limited background.

Significant care should be taken in making charts, graphs, and tables. You want to avoid making "pretty" charts that say nothing substantive. Hype is acceptable in advertising, but it is not relished by doctoral committees, or business managers or public policy experts expecting something concrete from which to make decisions and policies.

Alternatively, charts that are too difficult to understand or are overloaded with information will seriously limit the audience's receptivity to your thesis, paper or report. Senior-level managers and doctoral committee members may also chastise you for wasting their time plowing through your work. People listening as you present "busy" charts may spend all of their time trying to discern what the charts are showing and ignore what you are saying.

Remember, your goal is to produce a document that is readable by your target audience. That suggests that it is better to err on the side of having too many simple charts than to have too few complicated ones.

This is also an excellent opportunity to instill an image of your research goals into the minds of your audience. It gives you the chance to say, "My work is ready for immediate use in enhancing the business or the good of the general public."

Doing business in the global marketplace now demands that you know and use international units.

Imagine you are giving a scientific presentation to a group of engineers in a foreign country. You are quite proud of your findings, and you are sure that these strangers will embrace your ideas, for these ideas should significantly improve their competitiveness.

You open by saying, "We increased the burst pressure on our hose from 5000 psi to 8000 psi." You know they don't speak English so you wait for the interpreter to translate your message. When he or she is finished, you notice that there are blank stares looking up at you. "What did I do wrong?" you think to yourself. You continue, "We also reduced the weight per foot by 0.15 pounds." The interpreter tries again to convey your message. Again you see blank stares.

The interpreter does not want to embarrass you, so he allows you to continue. Somehow you get through your presentation based on the polite smiles from your audience. They don't ask any questions, for their culture demands that the audience make an effort to understand the information that the speaker is giving in their presentation.

As you prepare to leave, you wonder why no one asked for a sample of your product. You wait for someone to say something, but nothing happens. Your interpreter then thanks your host for allowing you to speak, and you all politely leave.

You recount your visit trying to discern what went wrong. The blank stares in the customers' faces are now haunting your mind. Then you realize that the puzzled expressions meant that these foreign customers had no idea what you were speaking about. They understand units such as bar, mega Pascal, meter, and kilogram — not pounds per square inch or foot.

You just received a tough lesson in communicating in the world marketplace, for you wasted a great deal of your corporation's resources to sponsor your foreign trip and produced no return on their investment. A little forethought could have made this a successful trip. You should have created charts and graphs using units that could be understood by your intended audience. This is also true for internal corporate reports where one must present findings in a manner that is usable by the corporation's global family membership.

The doctoral candidate is confronted with a similar situation when they have worked out their statistics but report their findings in a format that is foreign to their intended audience. The thesis review may find your committee members requiring you to get your data in the right format. Therefore, if you use the appropriate units and report in customary formats, your thesis, article or report is ready for the world marketplace.

> Develop your report to the highest standard of excellence needed for your potential audience and you only need to write your work once to meet the requirements of all media.

The doctoral student needs to write papers for coursework as if writing a portion of their doctoral thesis or dissertation. High-caliber papers offer sections that can be easily ported into the thesis or dissertation with minor adjustments.

Some people will tell you that a given report does not require a very high standard of accuracy, so you might offer your audience rough data or promise to correct it later. These statements are fine if you expect your work is to have only limited exposure to non-decision-making individuals and a brief shelf life. Today, it is imperative that you not get caught putting material in the public domain that you do not expect to find its way around the world. Technology is allowing your written word, voice and picture to be put up on the Internet within minutes of your talk. You only want to put out drafts to a handful of trusted people who are part of your development process.

If there is even a remote possibility that your work will land in front of a senior manager or might become a part of a retrievable database system, you need to make certain that this work represents your highest degree of performance. This technique will also give you the added ability to generate ancillary documents, presentations, and trade articles very quickly since the data is portable. It means that the doctoral candidate can quickly put together a thesis from research building blocks made in courses touching on his or her research area of interest.

In my last year at the DuPont Company, I was in the midst of preparing a technical paper to present to the Society of Automotive Engineers when I learned that another researcher could not honor a request to the Detroit Rubber Group, a subdivision of the Rubber Division of the American Chemical Society. I was in the midst of writing a paper for another society to be given near the same time as the second paper, so I found myself writing two technical papers on two different subjects to be presented within a two-week period.

The first paper was well underway, but the research on the second paper needed finalizing. The initial effort on the first paper took the form of writing the trade paper for the Society of Automotive Engineers within the guidelines of the company's internal technical report format. I, therefore, had a document that had portability and could be readily modified to meet restrictions placed on my findings by management and the legal department.

Since time was my worst enemy, I worked on the second article in a joint arrangement with another scientist who had conducted the research we intended to use to demonstrate the superiority of our product over a multinational competitor's product. We were a good team, for I understood the trade needs from my own research efforts; my coauthor understood our product's superior traits with supporting data.

I utilized the internal technical reporting system to lay out this second research paper in a short time period using the known information. My coauthor completed his internal measurements, and we produced the internal technical report, including all approvals for the presentation to the Detroit Rubber Group, in roughly six weeks.

Using the existing company technical reporting system as a template for an external research paper reduced the stress of developing a new paper quickly, as our effort became one of filling in the blanks. This system also allowed us to get a peer review of our efforts while we were still writing the paper. Therefore, we only needed to present a final draft to our management for approval. We made all of our management-suggested corrections in one day, for we had the paper on our own computer. We had little problem meeting our presentation schedule.

I had planned to give a last paper to close out my technical marketing and end-use research career with the DuPont Company in November of 1993, the month of my retirement. I was to give the same paper at the Fall' 93 meeting of the International Society of Industrial Fabric Manufacturers, as well as Textile World's "Textiles in Automotives" Fall' 93 Conference. However, there was a need to give an additional paper at the Textile World conference.

I took advantage of the portability of works done with powerful software on personal computers. By simply making minor modifications in the charts on behalf of my new audience, the second paper and its presentation charts were completed in a couple of hours. Thus, I gave two consecutive papers on two different subjects on the same day.

The key issues here are aiming your writing at the highest level of potential audiences and developing ancillaries on systems that offer you the maximum in portability.

Using Windows or Apple operating systems software eases the wear on your nerves.

One of the key elements in writing theses, technical papers, internal and trade presentations, and technical reports quickly is the portability of data between applications.

Suppose your boss asked you to make a presentation on your technical report findings to both management and operators at a couple of your plant sites. In generating your initial paper, you worked in the Microsoft Office framework where you made your tables in Excel and later you wished to compose your documents in WordPerfect. You can now exchange items between these high-end programs; therefore, if you saved your original work on a storage system, you can simply call it up and insert the charts you need. Today, you can work also between Apple and Windows versions of Word. Hence, having written your initial work at the highest possible level now offers you the flexibility to use cut-and-paste techniques to develop a host of targeted reports and presentations. This means the doctoral candidate can write a thesis quickly with information supplied from many sources that are compatible with Microsoft products.

To become proficient in generating quick reports or theses, you should consider obtaining a working knowledge of word processing, database, graphics, statistics, and spreadsheet programs running under the Windows or Apple format. This knowledge allows you to do in hours, with a high degree of accuracy, jobs that would take days to do without such programs.

Working with your data gives an excellent insight into reality.

Most people desire to have some status in life. As we work at our profession, we expect to be recognized for our contributions, and we want the perks that tell the public we have arrived. We use earned degrees, patents, publications and so on to gauge our value to the organization. But this ego-building has a downside that is very costly to the company. If we allow ego blindness to encourage us to merely get our assistants to rack up data and offer us only summaries, our corporation loses the quality of our expertise and our quickness at solving problems.

When you are working through your raw data, you develop a sense for what it says. You also recognize when it is insufficient to answer the questions posed to you by your research advisor or corporate management; if so, you can establish a new series of tests where needed.

You may find that little subtleties can go unnoticed in summaries that can be very significant in interpreting the data. The recognition of these subtleties can mean the difference between average and excellent research reports. Nevertheless, it is easy to have technicians and undergraduate students collect data and organize it into nice, neat charts. This takes less time on your part. If you have merely one or two pieces of data, this system is fine, but you may sacrifice those subtleties.

Whenever there is a considerable amount of data for analysis, you may find having your assistant do all of the tabulation helps these employees obtain a good appreciation of the test results, but it does little for you, the principal researcher. You gave away a golden opportunity to get an in-depth understanding of what the numbers and pictures convey. The impact of this knowledge loss is lessened when doctoral candidates become the high-powered technicians doing the data gathering. The concern is that the doctoral candidate becomes proficient at data-gathering and offering opinions with little progress towards the doctorate degree. It is very important that doctoral candidates do not allow themselves to become overly valued as technicians, which would make it difficult for their advisor to foster their graduation in a timely manner.

You will also find it rewarding to take the time to ensure your technicians or assistants are trained to understand your research effort. They should understand your test results, since it offers you an extra trained mind to comment on your findings. Technicians often see things that will elude your eyes, especially if the project is very large with many sets of data.

If you personally observe an experiment, you know the difference between fact and fantasy.

Some engineers and scientists may write up a work request for experiments then sit and await the results. Technicians often make notes on the report to describe what happens. If you are running a routine test, these notes may be more than adequate to meet your needs. However, if you are on the forefront of knowledge, there is no substitute for seeing the experiment run personally that may help you to recognize new directions hidden in the subtleties of the data.

This first-hand observation offers an opportunity to modify the test if something is wrong. It also gives an understanding of the details of the test effort and potential problems.

Your personal experience in observing test runs offers you a quantum leap in understanding when it comes time to analyze the data. You have a clear picture of the problem areas in your mind. It is also a key ingredient in the recipe for quick writing for doubt in your mind can encumber your ability to write. There is an adage that says, "Doubt is a veil over your mind, but confidence is the light that guides you through ignorance."

Analyzing your data today prevents tomorrow's confusion and anxiety.

The importance of understanding your data cannot be overemphasized in learning to write in a timely manner. Therefore, one must look for every opportunity to foster that understanding, including doing small things that reduce the complexity of the issues that are before us.

If you immediately write a few data analysis statements at the bottom of each sheet of data, you will find this data has instant value as a writing tool. It is also meaningful to other people who may view this effort. By adding these immediate assessments to your work, you have prevented reams of new data from turning into a mass of confusion.

Should you opt not to make an immediate assessment of the data, you may find yourself struggling to recall just what you were doing. Therefore, you have introduced doubt, and that turns your writing effort into a real chore. Making interim notes during the investigation provides a basis from which to take a holistic look at the information, regardless of whether the premises of your research remain the same.

A thoughtful data summary is a personification of your effort.

Writing is nothing more than using words to create a picture of an emotion in your mind. Text, tables, and charts are merely a materialization of your ideas. They give them life and make others more accepting of your feelings. Thus, an excellent summary of your research effort seeks to make your audience share in your conviction.

An excellent summary is a necessary item if you are to have a ghost of a chance at timely writing. This summary will allow you to write internal reports and presentations at the same time. With a word processing program such as WordPerfect or Word, statements from a research report can be copied to a presentation framework and minor modifications can be made to the information as necessary. This technique allows you to generate presentations for management or customers or university seminars very quickly.

If you admit, "I don't know," no one will make a fool of you.

One of the most difficult things for many people to do is to admit that they don't know everything. Somehow we believe we must be omnipotent, or we appear weak. This thinking is absolute suicide when it comes to quick writing, for you are no longer writing with a clear understanding of purpose. You are now moving from the realm of technical writing to fictional writing, for what you say may simply not be true.

Those with in-depth knowledge of your field will recognize your futile attempt at fiction in a nonfiction arena, and they may ask for your liberal interpretation of the facts. Senior managers and doctoral committee chairpersons may not be kind, should they find out that you misrepresented the facts.

If you point out that you don't know something but you will research it further at a later date, you may find it forms closure on questions and retains your credibility. If you say "I don't know," you have not committed a crime. If you say that you are continuing your research in this area to attempt to answer some difficult questions, that leaves the reader yearning for your next work. However, doctoral candidates should not find themselves saying "I do not know" for information that is expected of them too many times or they will lose credibility in the eyes of their doctoral committee members.

If you are a know-it-all, you may find your audience giving you enough rope to hang yourself and then taking great pleasure in your demise. Why lose your valuable credibility with ego blindness that may disappear in a few moments?

> Copying at least two sets of your report on a CD or removable hard drive and storing them in different secure locations eliminates writer's paranoia over the potential of your computer crashing or a natural disaster destroying your work.

Whenever we write very large reports, we find ourselves protecting this work in hard copies and electronic copies. We know that the potential for a disaster is always present, and we hate to think of our great writing effort being the victim of a disaster. Subtle pressures such as this weigh heavily on your mind when you are trying to write, they cloud your thinking; an impediment to quick writing. On the other hand, if you are not working on secure information, you might simply email copies to two different friends or family members living in different cities.

I am merely contending that you want to follow the old adage, "An ounce of prevention is worth a pound of cure."

> You cannot edit for yourself.

You may find that you are writing what you thought was in your mind, but what you typed into the computer might be something slightly different. Each time you reread the manuscript you picture what is in your mind versus what is really on the paper. You have two options to solve this problem.

Option one: You can allow the manuscript to sit in a drawer for some period of time until it is not at the forefront of your thinking. Then you may reread the manuscript with the mindset that it was written by someone else. You will most likely pick up many of the errors that you couldn't see while you were in the process of writing this manuscript. This technique adds a considerable amount of editing time to your producing a publishable work. You also run the risk that you do not recognize significant errors in your writing, so the quality of your final document may be substandard.

Option two: You can you use a professional editor with some background in the subject area in which you are writing. This professional will edit your document for plausibility and correct grammar. You want an editor who has some appreciation for the subject matter on which you are reporting. A grammarian may improve the flow of your manuscript, but there may be technical errors missed. This is not very productive, especially when you are attempting to produce manuscripts for publications at the doctoral level and for journals or books. If necessary, you may want to consider getting two people to read your manuscript, one to read for technical content and the other to correct your grammar.

> Accept that making corrections to both the content and the structure of your manuscript is the norm in producing a high-caliber publishable document.

Most people are not perfect writers. Therefore, they will make mistakes in drafting their manuscripts. In order to produce a high-quality manuscript, you need to be able to catch and correct these errors in your final document. Once these errors are identified, you must have a willingness to make these corrections to improve the final product. Ego blindness can be a death knell in this case for you may feel embarrassed about having to make corrections on issues that may be technically incorrect. Recalcitrance will only slow your writing process because your research advisor or corporate management is going to challenge you to make the necessary corrections to come up with a professional manuscript.

Most newspaper or electronic media people know well the value of editors who edit the works of reporters who are attempting to get a breaking news story written quickly. Publishing companies have editors who work with writers to elevate manuscripts to production quality. Hence, your receptivity to working with editors can make your document writing experience move along much faster. Keep in mind that your ultimate goal is to get your manuscript published or your doctoral thesis approved by your doctoral committee. If you stay focused on the goal, you will recognize that the editors are there to help you achieve your objective. Thus, once you defend your doctoral thesis, you should recognize that any corrections your doctoral committee gives you to make are only a minor obstacle between you and achieving your doctorate degree. You should then make these corrections aggressively and present the final manuscript to your committee chairperson.

Stay away from the naysayer.

I have learned over the years that quick writing starts with a belief in your own capabilities. If you believe you can write your doctoral thesis or article or book, chances are you can accomplish your goal with some assistance. If there is doubt about your ability to write, you may be leaving yourself open to procrastination. Hence, you want to stay away from people who make depressing comments on their inability to achieve goals, for it may be infectious.

I recall a person who had the ability to pass the doctoral level courses, but this person was horrified at the thought of writing the doctoral thesis. This conversation was changed quickly in the direction of my confidence in being able to write a doctoral thesis, so I never internalized thoughts of failure.

Self-discipline keeps you on task when pressing matters compete for your time.

If you are to get your writing task (thesis, report, article, or book) accomplished, you need self-discipline to stay on the job until it is completed. This means that you must prioritize things competing for your time or you might overwhelm yourself attempting to accomplish all of these tasks. If your goal is to earn a doctoral degree, you may have to give up watching sports, or other leisure activities. John C. Maxwell writes, "To develop a lifestyle of discipline, one of your first tasks must be to challenge and eliminate any tendency to make excuses" (Maxwell 129). Once you start to make excuses, you may already be on the path to becoming a permanent ABD, even though it is not apparent to you at the moment.

When the bell rings in you mind to start writing, then start. When the bell rings again in your mind to stop writing, then you must stop.

There are certain times in which you can sit in front of a computer and write very aggressively and productively on your manuscript. There are other times in which no matter how hard you attempt to write, nothing productive seems to come out even though you thought out your subject theme very well.

I like to think of this writer's cramp as a bell that rings in my mind that tells me when it is the right time to write. Then this bell rings again, telling me it is time to stop. Once the bell has rung to stop, it appears that my writing efforts suddenly become nonproductive, for the text that comes is substandard in a publishing arena. What I'm suggesting is that there may be periods in which you should write and there are those in which you should not attempt to write. If you are to accomplish your goal of writing your manuscript in a reasonable time, your focus should be on utilizing productive periods well. Writing only in your productive periods may improve your production of publishable caliber material because it leaves time to address lower priority items on your to-do list.

Do not equivocate on issues on which you are writing.

When you are equivocating on issues, you may find that it becomes a challenging effort to write because you are attempting to suppress your natural feelings. You may slow your own writing capacity down because you are attempting to translate your emotions into someone else's mindset.

When I was learning to write national commentaries under the tutelage of the late Pulitzer Prize winner Norman Lockman, he encouraged me to write based on my own feelings. He also wanted me to follow the data and not get bogged down following some erroneous emotions. I learned from Lockman that once I wrote based on my own style I could write national commentaries quickly. Prior to my study under Lockman, I had studied under the late Bill Johnson, who was publisher of the Charlotte Post. Johnson informed me to stop attempting to appease everyone in the audience. He said, "you must take a position on issues and catch the heat that accompanies your stances." Once I experienced the teachings of the two newspaper industry gentlemen above, my ability to write national opinion commentaries was greatly enhanced and I found a following of readers.

I found the above teachings from the newspaper industry worked very well in writing my doctoral thesis, for I was able to write things in a matter of days that may have taken other people weeks to accomplish. The added caveat is that you must write as a peer of your doctoral committee members if your hope is to get a doctoral degree. This means you must write on your research issues from your personal insights and not attempt to become a clone of your research advisor.

Chapter VII

Setting Priorities Frees Time to Write

Since completing and defending the thesis or dissertation is the pinnacle of the doctoral degree quest, the counsel of busy people who completed the degree will offer additional insight on how to avoid succumbing to the mortal sin of procrastination or the fatalism of self-doubt.

High School Principal

I asked a principal of a high school to give his recipe for completing his doctoral degree. He said that he and two other principals in his cohort took two courses each semester and in the summer to get the coursework finished as quickly as possible. This scheme allowed them to complete the doctoral degree in three years.

I then asked how he avoided not giving up when the going got tough. He replied, "Quitting wasn't an option!" He argued that you get nothing for starting and stopping. Furthermore, it would have been unfair to put his wife and children through the stress of his degree quest for no reason.

When I chatted with this young principal I felt an aura of *determination* that pervades his conversation. I quickly recognized that completion of a task has a very high priority in his approach to life. If he was looking to become a superintendent in the future, it was clear that he has the principal's experience and now the doctoral degree in education leadership.

Community College Administrator

I asked a lady who is an administrator at a community college about her doctoral degree quest. She made it clear that completion of her degree was a given, and revealed that nine of eleven people in her friends circle had completed the doctoral program. Her revelation on her friends' completions really grabbed my attention, considering one might have expected something closer to a 50 percent completion rate, which is the national average. I surmised that *peer pressure* offered this lady significant motivation to complete the degree in order to maintain her social status with her peers.

Major University Administrator

I asked an administrator at a major university how she managed to complete her dissertation. She revealed that she was the mother of three young children during the period that she wrote her dissertation, which she wrote two hours everyday after attending to the needs of her children. It was obvious that she did not attempt to use these children's well-being to justify procrastination.

As I looked into this lady's eyes, it was obvious that she was the stereotypical "supermom." Her degree completion goal was paramount, so she figured out how to incorporate her writing assignment around her motherly duties.

Degree Completion Plan for the Busy Person

a) See determination as your mantra, because quitting is not an option,

b) Association with doctorate degree holders for peer pressure is good,

c) Integrate your degree assignments into your daily routine with your family, and

d) Keep plugging away until you hear your advisor call you "Doctor."

Advice to a Friend Thinking about Beginning the Doctoral Quest

A thirty-something friend who is in an administrative position sought my advice in an email on pursuing a doctoral degree. He wrote,

> ". . . I would one day love to earn a PhD or EdD. . . . I sometimes wonder how I would ever have time to earn a doctorate with all that my wife and I have going on (kids in school, church, full-time work, etc.). But I believe that it would be a benefit to my career in higher ed. More than that, it would be the fulfillment of a dream. Actually, I wanted to be a physician (MD) when I was a child but after deciding not to pursue medicine for various reasons and learning more about other types of terminal degrees, I felt that I would one day pursue some kind of doctorate degree. It seems to me that if one is planning to work while pursuing a doctorate, one must have the "right" kind of job that provides flexibility and perhaps even provides some access to research and scholarly opportunities. I think that being here at XXXX gives me the latter, but the actual time required to do my job would be a challenge in pursuing doctoral work. Not sure how this will all play out, but I trust God to direct me. If you have suggestions or thoughts, please share. . ."

Heretofore the comments have assumed that the doctoral students have already started the doctoral degree quest. The above email offers an opportunity to help shape the mindset on the factors leading to the affirmative decision to pursue the doctoral quest. I responded,

In the new book I am writing the last chapter will address the issues you bring up. I asked some folks who are as busy as you are how they got it done. I have not written that chapter yet. Nevertheless there are some issues you must control.

> 1. The doctoral level is very different from BS and MS level. Your role is to think like a peer of your advisor. If you think like a dutiful graduate student, they will treat you like that.
>
> 2. Set up an arrangement where you can take two courses each semester. Perhaps, courses online on Saturday. You want to get the required courses and qualifying examination out of the way ASAP.
>
> 3. Write all research papers as if they are your thesis or dissertation. You can come back later and cut and paste.
>
> 4. Be sure your advisor has stature in the department. This means that person can manage tomfoolery on your committee if two members have disdain for one another and you become their whipping boy. Topics on which you all agree will not get knocked down by other more powerful members of the department.
>
> 5. Pick only committee members that like one another. This avoids the problems hinted in number 4.
>
> 6. You must believe in yourself even when things look like they are going to hell in a hand basket. Self doubt will have you second guessing the need for the quest, so you may stop in mid-stream and get nothing for your time and effort.
>
> 7. You must be honest and tell your wife that this is a very tough quest and you will need her support to finish it. She will comfort you when you are toying with quitting.
>
> 8. Pick a thesis or dissertation topic on which you have some knowledge and it is a very doable effort. Your goal

is to add some small amount to the body knowledge and not try to revolutionize your field.

9. Write an analysis on each piece of data that you collect, so later it will be meaningful. If you wait until the last minute to attempt to analyze a lot of data, you may find yourself in a quagmire.

10. The mortal sin of the doctoral quest is procrastination. Whatever you do keep away from an enchantment with procrastination or you will find yourself an All But Dissertation student for eternity.

Summary

Many American black communities are in the midst of an education crisis that is encumbering their socioeconomic progress. The Manhattan Institute reports, "Only 51% of all black [high school] students and 52% of all Hispanic students graduate, and only 20% of all black students and 16% of all Hispanic students leave high school college-ready" (Greene, 2003). The Education Trust shares that under 30 percent of the undergraduate black students graduate from college in six years. The Council of Graduate Schools reports, "White students have the highest cumulative ten-year [doctoral degree] completion rate at 55%, compared to 51% for Hispanic Americans, 50% for Asian Americans, and 47% for African Americans" (PhD Completion Project, 2008). On the other hand, the Reentry Policy Council writes, "around 60 percent of black male high-school dropouts now in their mid-30s have prison records." (Western, 2003). A key ingredient in eliminating this black American educational nightmare may be to develop "Neighborhood Role Models" that neighborhood people can see and interact with daily. Thus, we have developed a writing mindset and template to help future neighborhood role models and mainstream people write their dissertation or doctoral thesis in a timely manner.

President Barack Obama is the greatest role model of academic achievement for African Americans. However, the evolution of neighborhood role models who have completed doctoral degrees may re-enfranchise the pursuit of academic excellence in many black communities. The neighborhood role models' presence may help to remove any mysticism surrounding doctoral degree holders and inspire people of all ages to pursue the doctorate. The doctoral degree carries the global symbolism of academic excellence, so black neighborhood role models will signify that there is untapped human resource potential in black communities.

Appendix

Research and Technical Report Writing Template

[Project Name]

[Your Name]

[Project Completion Date]

Vision

Write how you see things tomorrow once your target audience responds to your research findings. It should be written in a maximum of three sentences.

Abstract

Summarize your research findings to justify to the reader her or his need to spend time to read your report. In an industrial report you give senior management results on which to make business decisions because they may not wish to read your entire report.

Introduction

Give a literature review that establishes the need for your research in your thesis or dissertation. In an industrial report, you offer justification for using corporate funds and equipment to do your research.

Premises

Present assumptions that establish your initial position. They are especially important in theoretical works. These assumptions may prove to be wrong in the development of your research.

Objectives

Goals that you intend to meet with your research. It is very important that you do not attempt to restate goals to match your findings without the approval of your doctoral committee chairperson or your industrial project manager.

Discussion

Sketch out your tests to show that they are credible measures in the eyes of your peers. Give data and discuss its meaning to your audience. You may want to highlight that you have a new discovery, new insight, entrance into a new market, or ability to maintain an existing market position under competitive threat.

Summary

Highlight the findings in your research effort and offer your analysis of what they suggest.

Conclusion

Offer what insights you concluded from the analysis of your data. Give future directions suggested by your research. Sometimes this section is merged with the summary section.

Appendix

Present detailed calculations, statistical information, and so on that does not need to be in the body of the thesis or industrial report.

Works cited

Give a bibliography where readers can find any works that you cite.

Works Cited

All But Dissertation (ABD) Policies. (1995, May 8). Retrieved 12 23, 2007, from Carnegie Mellon University Doctoral Candidate Policies for All But Dissertation (ABD) : http://www.cmu.edu/policies/documents/ABD.html

Bureau, U. C. (2006, 11 22). *U.S. and World Population Clocks - POPClocks*. Retrieved December 22, 2007, from U.S. Census Bureau: http://www.census.gov/main/www/popclock.html

Chamberlin, J. (1999, February). *Faculty offer clues to clearing the 'all-but-dissertation' hurdle*. Retrieved December 23, 2007, from APA Monitor Online: http://apa.org/monitor/feb99/hurdle.html

Doctoral Degree Awards to African Americans Reach Another All-Time High. (2006). Retrieved July 15, 2008, from The Journal of Blacks in Higher Education: http://www.jbhe.com/news_views/50_black_doctoraldegrees.html

Greene, J. P. (2003, September). *Education Working Paper*. Retrieved May 17, 2009, from Manhattan Institute for

Policy Research: http://www.manhattan-institute.org/html/ewp_03.htm

Gravois, J. (2007, April 6). *Trapped by Education.* Retrieved July 15, 2008, from The Chronicle of Higher Education: http://chronicle.com/free/v53/i31/31a01001.htm

Healy, B. (2008, April 18). *Bank of America cuts back on loans - Ends private finance program for students.* Retrieved July 15, 2008, from The Boston Globe: http://www.boston.com/business/articles/2008/04/18/bank_of_america_cuts_back_on_loans?mode=PF

Historical National Population Estimates: July 1, 1900 to July 1, 1999. (2000, 6 28). Retrieved December 22, 2007, from U.S. Census Bureau : http://www.census.gov/popest/archives/1990s/popclockest.txt

Hoffer, T. B., Welch, V. (2006, March). Retrieved July 15, 2008, from National Science Foundation: http://www.nsf.gov/statistics/infbrief/nsf06312/nsf06312.pdf

Jaschik, S. (2007, 12 17). *How to Cut Ph.D. Time to Degree.* Retrieved December 24, 2007, from Inside Higer Ed: http://www.insidehighered.com/news/2007/12/17/phd

Kotter, J. P. (1996). *Leading Change.* Boston, Massachusetts: Harvard Business School Press.

Lovitts, B. E., Nelson, C. (2000, Nov/Dec). *The Hidden Crisis in Graduate Education: Attrition From Ph.D. Programs.* Retrieved December 24, 2007, from Academe Online: http://www.aaup.org/AAUP/pubsres/academe/2000/ND/Feat/lovi.htm

Maxwell, J. C. (1999). Challenge Your Excuses. In J. C. Maxwell, *The 21 Indispensable Qualities of A Leader* (p. 129). Nashville: Thomas Nelson, Inc.

Miller, S. a. (1993). Aramid Transverse Filament Properties and Hose Fitting Retention. *Detriot Rubber Group a subdivision fo the Rubber Division of the American Chemical Society.*

Ogden, E. H. (2007). *Complete Your Dissertation or Thesis in Two Semester or Less.* Lanham, Maryland: Rowman & Littlefield Publishers, Inc.

PhD Completion Project: Analysis of Baseline Demographic Data, Vo l u m e 4 (2008, July). Retrieved May 17, 2009, from Communicator Council of Graduate Schools: http://www.cgsnet.org/portals/0/pdf/comm_2008_07.pdf

Terletzky, A. (2004, February 4). *NYU combats Ph.D. dropout rate.* Retrieved December 24, 2007, from Washington Square News: http://media.www.nyunews.com/media/storage/paper869/news/2004/02/04/UndefinedSection/Nyu-Combats.Ph.d.Dropout.Rate-2390562.shtml

Thurgood, L., Golladay, M., & & Hill, S. (2006, June). *U.S. Doctorates in the 20th Century.* Retrieved 12 22, 2007, from National Science Foundation: http://www.nsf.gov/statistics/nsf06319/pdf/nsf06319.pdf

Western, B. (2003, December 1). *Lawful Re-entry.* Retrieved May 17, 2009, from The American Prospect: http://www.prospect.org/cs/articles?article=lawful_reentry

About the Author

Sherman N. Miller has been an adjunct professor of mathematics at West Chester University, Widener University, St. Joseph's University, Immaculata University, Neuman University, and Strayer University. Dr. Miller is a retired visiting instructor of mathematics at Delaware State University where his expertise was teaching mathematics from basic through business calculus to background deficient students coming from inner city backgrounds. He has a doctoral degree in education leadership from the University of Delaware where his doctoral thesis offered a plan to increase the pass rate for background deficient students in finite mathematics and business calculus at Delaware State University.

Dr. Miller is currently developing a neighborhood role model program where his focus is to encourage African Americans and other minorities to pursue the doctoral degree with the goal of altering de facto redlining of human resource potential in inner city America.

Index

A

B

C

D

E

F

G

H

I

J

K

L

M

N

O

P

Q

R

S

T

U

V

W

www.ingramcontent.com/pod-product-compliance
Lightning Source LLC
LaVergne TN
LVHW020642100826
845148LV00012B/2306